A Decorator's Secrets

A Decorator's Secrets
Carolyn Warrender

HarperCollins*Publishers*

For a very special sister, Bella

First published in the United States of America in 2000 by Abbeville Press

First Edition

10   9   8   7   6   5   4   3   2   1

Library of Congress Cataloging-in-Publication Data

Warrender, Carolyn.
    Decorator's secrets / by Carolyn Warrender.
        p.   cm.
    Includes index.
    ISBN 0–78920–615–3
    1. Interior decoration. 2. House furnishings. I. Title.
NK2115.W23 1999
747–dc21

99-42400
CIP

Every effort has been made to ensure the information in this book is correct. However, we cannot assume any responsibility or liability caused by reliance upon the accuracy of such information. Specialist advice should be obtained where necessary and local building and planning regulations checked before starting any work.

Author acknowledgments

I would like to thank everyone at HarperCollins*Publishers* for all their work in producing this book. Special thanks go to my Editor, Becky Humphreys; Clare Baggaley, Mabel Chan and Kathryn Gammon in the Design Department and Laura Wickenden for the photographs in my home. Many people have helped and contributed to this book. In particular many thanks to Lucy Peel, Sarah Alexander, Glenn Milner, Adi Strieder, Perry Butler and Nigel Stubbings. Writing this book would not have been possible without the support and understanding of my husband, Francis; my children, Jamie and Geordie; all my family; and five special people – Sue Hoggard, Jill Strieder, Caroline Ward, Kaye Grosvenor and Tessa Stickland.

contents

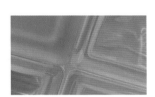

introduction

I think that a well-designed house is like a favorite pair of jeans: a combination of comfort, practicality and good looks. Just as we feel confident when we know we are well dressed, it is no different when it comes to how we view our homes. The question is: how, if you are not a professional, can you achieve the home of your dreams?

Stores, magazines and television programs offer great advice and inspirational ideas that always seem magically to fit together. However, when it actually comes to realizing these ideas, it never seems as easy.

Most people go to the hairdresser and don't attempt to cut their hair themselves. Doing something you have not been trained to do can be expensive in the long run, and we have all paid the price of trying to do something on the cheap!

Professional interior designers are often viewed with a certain skepticism. Common misconceptions are that interior designers will impose their "style" and ignore your ideas, and that using a professional will cost a lot of money. I believe that a good designer should always listen to what a client wants, and that his or her expertise will prevent expensive mistakes. An added bonus of using a professional is a knowledge of where to access products and services.

For over 25 years I have been involved in creating homes for people to live in, working both as a decorator and as a designer of home furnishing collections. Every project presents a different challenge, and my work as a designer is constantly evolving as tastes change and new products are developed.

In order to bring my experience and expertise to a wide audience, I have developed a series of Home Design Workshops. Here, I teach the basic principles of interior design and share my tricks of the trade, aiming to give people inspiration and information to use when decorating their own homes. It was the popularity of these workshops that gave me the idea to write this decorating course. Through it I hope to teach you how to be the interior designer of your own home and to give you the flair, knowledge and confidence to make the best of your ideas. Designing and decorating a home is rather like doing a jigsaw puzzle. You have all the different pieces in front of you, and the trick is to fit them together. But, first some basic rules to think about before you start.

CAROLYN WARRENDER

▶ **Develop the confidence to transform even a basic utility room with bold colors and specialty fittings.**

psychology of the home

I am often asked what is the most important aspect of my interior design work. For me it has to be that we are happy in our own home. This may sound simple, but people often tell me that they are unable to relax at home. On closer analysis, this is usually because of their surroundings, such as the color of a room, or how the furnishings are arranged.

Start by playing the truth game with yourself. If you are someone who loves walks in the country and the outdoor life, you are unlikely to be happy in an environment decorated in a stark, minimal, contemporary style. Visualize a scene where you are totally relaxed, and work out what creates this atmosphere. Does your home reflect any of this? If not, try incorporating some of these images into your decorating scheme.

Interior design is not just about choosing paint, fabrics and curtain styles. Open your eyes to the deeper meaning of the home, and how your surroundings affect you. Analyze your response to color and the effect certain colors have on the way you feel. Take the time to learn about Feng Shui, and you will be amazed at the difference that just moving furniture around a room can have.

Be honest and have the courage to make changes. Express yourself and don't be a slave to the latest fashion just for the sake of having something new. Never begin a job with preconceptions. Although you need to establish a broad framework, a room evolves and develops as time progresses.

what you have...

Before you start to plan a decorating scheme, it is important to assess what you already have that will need to be incorporated into your plans. It is rarely possible to start with a blank canvas.

Whether you are moving or just redecorating, walk around your home and take a good look at all your possessions. Sometimes we are so used to seeing something in the same place, we can forget it actually exists. Make notes, take snapshots and consider whether you can move any furniture or pictures to another room. Here again, have the courage to get rid of anything you don't like.

Look at how many rooms you have in your home and what they are used for. Are you making the best use of all the space? For example, rarely used spare rooms can become home offices, and, if you have a dining room, consider whether it could be used to extend your living room. This foundation work is essential, since once decorating starts it can be costly to make major changes.

A bath positioned under a window can be a wonderful place to lie and find inspiration from the views outside.

A child's choice of blue and red can be interpreted in matching checks and stripes. Note the oar used as a curtain rod!

Stunning, bright patterns are balanced here by plain yellow walls and anchored by a large picture above the bed. The riot of color is balanced with plain but original furniture and lighting.

...what you want

Think about why you are making changes to your home and what you want to achieve from them. It could be that you are changing your lifestyle, or that you are just renovating tired paintwork.

Think about how you use your home. Are you there during the day or just in the evening? Does the decoration have to be practical because you have small children? Do you like entertaining? All factors such as these have to be taken into account.

As your plans progress, your confidence will increase, and you will discover skills you never knew you had. If there are others in your household, listen to their ideas. With gentle guidance children

blossom if allowed to express themselves. Talk to friends too: someone who knows you and your home may well be able to look at your ideas from a more objective viewpoint, though ask someone whom you feel has similar taste.

Arguments with partners are very common when redecorating, and I have witnessed many near-divorces resulting from differences of opinion. Experience has taught me how to compromise when there is a clash of ideas. Everyone has a favorite room. It can be any room in the house. For my husband, Francis, it is the living room, where he loves to read and listen to music. For me, it is the bathroom, where I can escape, shut the door and forget the world outside.

An old screen panel makes an unusual but eye-catching headboard.

Each of you should be able to use your own scheme in "your" room. In this way it will be much easier to agree on the other rooms in the house, as each partner will have a room he or she is totally happy with. A fatal error is for both partners to have contrasting input into the same room – the result is inevitably disastrous!

Another consideration is individual reaction to color. My research into color analysis has resulted in some interesting conclusions. Color can be divided into "cool" and "warm" shades: cool shades have a blue base, while warm shades have a yellow base. Our natural skin, eye and hair color determine which base we tend to prefer. Put simply, if our coloring is cool we tend to respond better to cool-based colors, and likewise for warm coloring. Applying these theories to the colors we choose for our home can result in a more harmonious living environment.

A photograph taken on vacation can inspire you to create a Mediterranean-style cream and terra-cotta room.

Different shades of blues and greens work together to create a cool color scheme.

setting your plans in motion

I cannot emphasize enough the importance of good and careful planning before you start. Just as an interior designer takes time to talk to a client and take a brief, so you must learn to take your own brief.

Think about schedules, budgets, planning and setting realistic goals, and whether you need to call in any experts. It is essential to get everything right before you start. Economies on time at this stage usually result in time lost, to say nothing of the expense, at a later stage.

When planning your decorating schemes, take the time to visit as many stores as possible, and read every book and magazine you can find. In stores ask for samples, and cut pictures from magazines to start piecing the jigsaw puzzle together.

Take time to think through your plans objectively in a quiet place surrounded by things that inspire you.

individual style

Many interior designers are recognized for their individual style. My own work tends to be a bit more eclectic and less defined. I like to work with and develop each client's own individual style, and then, when I have completed a job, I would like to think that no one knows I have been there!

A house should always have humor, so don't worry if something looks a bit out of place. Quite often it is these little quirky touches which give a home its individuality. I am not a fan of decorating by numbers. It is virtually impossible to create a true particular "style" and the end result can look very contrived.

A true home follows the progression and evolution of the lives of the people who live there. Successful interior design should be a reflection of who you and your family are.

using this book

The book is divided into four main sections, backed up by a useful measurement guide, source list and index.

● **mastering the basics:** a workshop to help you understand and make the most of your room. Planning techniques and the use of color are explained in detail.

● **the raw materials:** an in-depth, practical and inspirational look at decorating materials and their uses.

● **interior design masterclass:** 12 different rooms illustrating in detail how the schemes were planned and executed.

● **troubleshooting:** a comprehensive question and answer session solving common decorating dilemmas.

This decorating course will give you an insight into how a professional interior designer works. All of the projects and photographs are taken in real homes – many of them in my own house!

Never think your decorating is complete when you put down your paintbrush. It has only just begun.

◊ **Involve the whole family in the design and decorating process. Here, Francis, Jamie and Geordie are hard at work stripping wallpaper in our hall.**

Carolyn Warrender

mastering the basics

understanding a room

Before starting to decorate a room, it is vital to allow time to take stock. Assess the existing space.

Consider how the room is used, its function. Is it used primarily for work, rest or play? Do you need it to be informal or formal, elegant or casual? Which members of the family use it the most, when, and for what? Certain parts of the house – kitchens and hallways – are in use all day, and kitchens in particular may be used for more than one function (cooking and eating). Bedrooms, however, are mainly used mornings and evenings, while living rooms may only be used in the evening. Write your information down, and use it to think carefully about possible designs.

How you use the space in a room and group the furniture will depend very much on its planned function. For example, with a playroom you may wish to leave a wide open central area for games, but with a dining room you will want to fill this space with a table. Similarly, in a living room you will need an area for sitting and chatting, but you may also wish to set aside a space for a desk.

Once you have established these basic facts, look at the physical characteristics of the room, its size and scale. The proportions – height, width and length – the size of the windows, as well as shape will all need to be taken into account when planning a design scheme. Don't be restricted by how the room currently looks – often there is more than one way to arrange furniture. It is easier to get a true sense of the proportions and scale of a room if it is empty. So clear out all distracting furniture and look at the bare bones of the room.

This is the time to take note of such factors as where the light falls and practical considerations such as the location of radiators, telephone and cable outlets, and electrical sockets. If any of these need moving this is the time to do it, before you start decorating.

Simple wooden kitchen units with plain, muted-colored walls are all that are needed when a room has a strong architectural feature like this arched window. The curved faucet discreetly echoes the curve of the window.

architectural features

Good architectural features are a bonus that should be celebrated, so if there are any strong features such as an attractive fireplace, interesting paneled door or sweeping floor-to-ceiling windows, emphasize them by making them the focal point in the room around which everything else is planned. Also, look out for interesting niches,

decorative cornices, paneling and dado rails. These can all be emphasized when decorating by being picked out in contrasting or darker colors.

Sometimes the architectural features of a room are so pronounced that they create instant character. This character could come from a room's shape, for example, if it has a steeply sloping or extremely high ceiling, or from its construction; beams are a good example of this. Again, let these features inspire and guide your decorative decision making.

Low beams may suggest a cozy cottage scheme, with plenty of warm colors and deep comfortable sofas. Sloping ceilings are more of a challenge. They can be painted in contrasting colors to emphasize the shapes to look almost sculptural, or visually lifted by being painted one simple light color. Very tall ceilings can look formal, but they can also look cold so the clever use of moldings or tricks, such as breaking up the space with an unusual arrangement of pictures can improve the room immeasurably.

Many houses have had all trace of architectural features stripped. If this is to your taste then emphasize the cool clear space with a few chic contemporary pieces of furniture. However, if you find such a space characterless, then simply treat it as a blank canvas and add as much character as you like. As it is possible to buy every type and period of architectural feature, you can really let your imagination run riot, and create any look from New England rustic to English Georgian elegance.

left **A spiral staircase can be used to great effect when space is at a premium. Paint it in a dark color if it will be a focal point. Rooms will look larger if the stair-case is painted to match the walls.**

right **The cornice details are picked out in a contrasting color to highlight the decorative design. This can also have the effect of lowering the ceiling in a high room.**

the importance of lighting

Lighting is not as immediately noticeable as color or pattern in a room; however, it is one of the most important elements in any design scheme. If the lighting is not right it does not matter how much time, effort and expense you have put into decorating, this will all simply be wasted. Without the right lighting you will never be able to achieve the effect you are looking for.

The direction the room faces will affect the amount of natural light it receives, when it gets it, its intensity, and the overall warmth. Also the size, shape and position of windows will have a bearing on how light is allowed in and where it falls. Make good use of any natural light. Once you have worked out what times of day a room gets direct sunlight, organize your furniture to take advantage of it, placing chairs where they will catch the sun.

In rooms where practical activities take place, such as kitchens and bathrooms, some of the lighting needs to be bright and directed. A kitchen needs some strategically placed task lights to cast light directly onto where you are working, while in the bathroom the mirror over the sink needs to be brightly lit.

However, in rooms which primarily exist for leisure activities – entertaining, chatting, watching television and general socializing – you only need ambient or mood lighting that will cast a gentle background glow. You are aiming for an effect which is both flattering and intimate, and to achieve this you will need a balance of table, standard and wall lights. Avoid using an overhead light if possible, as the illumination it casts always has a deadening effect, capable of killing atmosphere and conversation in equal measures.

Tall standard lamps with adjustable heads are useful. Their heads can be dipped, when all that is required is background lighting, or adjusted to give a direct light for reading. Dimmer switches are useful and, combined with separate switches for individual light sources, you can adjust the light to your requirements. The bulbs you choose will also have a bearing on the quality of light they produce. There is a huge choice of bulbs, from "daylight" bulbs, which cast a slightly cold, white light, to the more usual tungsten bulbs, which produce a warm, yellow light.

A single table lamp provides focused light for reading, and can be emphasized by well chosen accessories.

The clear roof light adds to the pool of natural light flooding in through the glass wall, and is reflected on the stainless steel surfaces.

developing your own style

Some people are born with an innate sense of style, others have to work at it. However, even people with a very strong individual look in terms of dress and hair may find the prospect of decorating a large room rather daunting. Also, unless you live on your own, there are the ideas and opinions of your partner to take into account. Designing by committee may produce rather bland results, but it is important to end up with a room you are both happy with.

The most obvious sources of inspiration are books, magazines and friends' houses. However, beware of copying a look verbatim since it will never feel truly yours. Instead pick and mix ingredients that you find appealing.

When you see a room that you find especially attractive, try to analyze what exactly it is that has caught your eye. Is it the color, the fabrics and patterns, pictures or style of furniture? It takes practice to be able to "break down" the look of a room into its constituent elements, but once you are able to do it you will find it an invaluable skill.

The minimal discipline of Japanese style can be softened by the use of a traditional but simple wooden table.

Most important of all is not to allow yourself to feel intimidated. There are no rules, so if you want to mix periods, combining furniture or fabrics that are fiercely modern with antiques, or rustic with sophisticated, then go ahead. Similarly, there is no reason why you should not mix quirky, ethnic pieces with traditional pieces you find locally.

The design and period of the house or even the shape and proportions of a room may direct you towards a certain decorating theme or style. A space full of clean sharp angles and lines has a very different feel from one full of sensuous curves, and it may cry out for a very contemporary look. Above all, give yourself time to get the "feel" of a room before starting work. If you can bear it, pare down your room to the bare minimum and live with it in this state for a few months. You will then have time to consider how you use the room. Remember too that once decorated, the basic framework of a room will continue to evolve as you start to use it.

A floor-to-ceiling mirror doubles the space in a room. Extra reflection is created with mirror glass used as the picture frame.

Circular mirrors in varying sizes for specific requirements work well together in this bathroom.

increasing space

Mirrors are an extremely useful weapon in the decorator's armory. They can be used to play all sorts of tricks with space and light. For example, the clever placing of a large mirror within a room will instantly make it look twice as large, and also twice as bright.

Long narrow rooms particularly benefit from the addition of a big mirror. The most difficult space can be transformed if one wall is covered in a huge mirror, effectively disguising the awkwardness of the room by doubling its visual size.

Many older houses have hallways where mirrors work tremendously well, opening up the space and making the area lighter and more welcoming at the same time. An excellent place to put the mirror is immediately above the radiator, preferably to the same width.

A room with a particularly dramatic or attractive view can be enhanced simply by hanging a large mirror on the wall opposite the window to bring the view into the room, thereby doubling its impact and really bringing the room to life.

making a plan

identifying key requirements

When assessing requirements, it is helpful to divide them up into two sections – practicalities and aesthetics. You should then look at these in light of your budgetary considerations.

Take your time compiling these lists, because getting things right at the outset can save a great deal of effort, upheaval and expense later on.

Under the practicalities heading consider whether any work needs doing on the essential structure of your home: heating, lighting, plumbing, soundproofing (for example, double glazing) and insulation. Then make a list of any repairs that are required. Once all of these elements have been taken into consideration you can move on to thinking about what you need to make the room work for you, either as an individual or as part of a family.

Among the aesthetic requirements you may want to consider is the overall style that you might like and whether this affects any existing features. Consider in detail the lighting, surface finishes, flooring, fabrics, patterns, furniture and color. Also think about storage, and whether you would like a clutter-free look or if you like to be surrounded by some of your possessions.

When your lists are complete you can get quotes for any work which requires a professional, such as plumbing or electrical wiring, then work out the rough costs of decorating materials and any new furniture you may want. When you have all the figures look at them in relation to your budget. Now is the time to revise your plans if they go over budget – once work starts any changes will be costly and, inevitably, extra costs are bound to be incurred as work progresses.

design and function

One of the most famous architects of the twentieth century, Le Corbusier, said: "A house is a machine for living in." In other words, however beautiful it looks, if

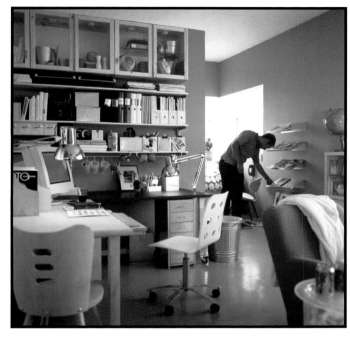

left A modern, streamlined kitchen combines function and design with a mix of open and closed storage.

right This small workspace benefits from open storage where everything is accessible.

The use of a glass table top makes this dual-purpose kitchen seem wider and reflects the light source from the large window.

it is impractical or uncomfortable you will never feel truly relaxed or at home in it. It must work smoothly and logically.

Of all the rooms in the house this is especially true of the kitchen, where ergonomics are especially important. Research has shown that while a cook prepares food he or she moves constantly between the oven, refrigerator and sink. It follows, therefore, that if these items are arranged in easily reachable positions the effort involved in cooking is considerably lessened. The optimum arrangement is that of a triangle, with the oven, refrigerator and sink all sitting in one corner.

Like most rooms in the house, a kitchen performs more than one function. It is now not just a place where food is prepared, but a social center too, and this social aspect should not be neglected.

While working out how a room is used is especially vital for a kitchen or bathroom, it is no less important for any other part of the house. The function of a room will determine your approach to decoration, and will also have a bearing on how people move around that room. This movement of people around a room is referred to as circulation, and getting the circulation plan right will help your home run smoothly and happily. For example, when organizing the furniture in the living room, try to avoid a layout that means that anyone walking into the room to sit down has to cross in front of the television, thus interrupting others' viewing. Also beware of positioning sofas or tables where you will have to squeeze past them to open and close the curtains or to switch on lamps. This will soon become a source of enormous irritation.

making a sample board

Long before you embark on decorating or even deciding upon a scheme, start collecting anything and everything that might provide inspiration or help you crystallize your likes and dislikes.

These items could range from photographs torn out of magazines to scraps of material, an *objet trouvé*, such as a shell or pebble from the beach, or even a piece of pottery which suggests a color or an atmosphere. Try to carry a small notebook and pen with you, so that you can jot down ideas as they come to you. You may, for example, be wandering around a department store and be struck by some display.

Store your finds in a big box and, once you feel you have enough, spread them out and examine them carefully. You are likely to find that certain colors, styles or themes predominate. These will help you decide upon a look for the room.

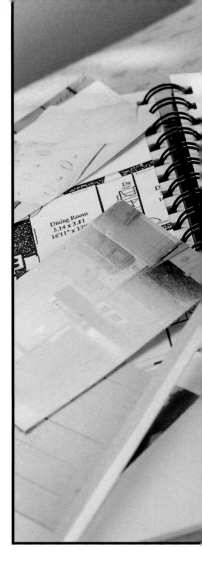

using swatches and samples

Once you have worked out what sort of overall look you are aiming for, then start putting together a sample board. This will allow you to make your imagined look a reality.

You will need a good selection of paint color samples (handpainted ones are always more accurate than the printed versions), wallpaper samples, fabric swatches and pieces of carpet. Take photographs of any rugs or items of furniture that have caught your eye or that you already possess, as well as of the room seen from different angles and at different times of day – preferably empty of furniture.

To work out which material, paper or paint will look good and where, do not simply try to imagine it in place – actually stick or pin your sample up *in situ*. It is impossible to make any decision on colors simply by relying on the manufacturer's tiny paint swatch, so paint pieces of white posterboard with your shortlist of possible colors and hang them on the wall.

Look at all your choices in different lights: first thing in the morning, at dusk, and under artificial light. See how they go together and, if something is not quite working

A loose-leaf notebook expands to take samples. Remember that any color chosen will always look darker when used in large quantities.

carry on experimenting with different samples and combinations, until you hit upon the definitive mix that brings your ideas to life.

measuring up

It is vital to draw up a scaled plan on graph paper of the room you are planning to decorate in order to work out required quantities of materials, such as paint, paper, carpets and so on, but more importantly to allow you to experiment with the room's layout, for example where best to position the furniture.

On your floor plan you should mark the width, length and height of the room, then draw in any fixed items such as doors (including the way they open), windows, fireplaces, alcoves, and radiators, finally adding electrical sockets, and telephone and television outlets.

Accuracy is all important, especially if you intend to allow carpetfitters or curtain makers to work from your plan, so double-check every measurement carefully. Next, cut out scale shapes of your furniture. By moving these shapes around you can work out the optimum layout and discover potential hitches, such as finding you do not have enough room to open the refrigerator when someone is sitting at the table.

Once you have decided on a potential layout, use a separate piece of tracing paper as an overlay on which to draw possible circulation plans.

planning lighting

It is vital to get a room's lighting right, as much for the sake of safety – for example, in a kitchen – as for ambience. Consider how much natural light the room receives at different times of the day. This may well vary between seasons. For example, in winter the sun sets earlier and sits lower in the sky, which may mean that a room which is bathed in light in the summer becomes quite gloomy during the winter months. Looking at a room around 9 P.M. during the summer can be a good indication of afternoon winter light.

△ **Take into account where the natural light source falls in a room.**

Think about what kind of artificial light you wish to use. This will depend to a large degree on the room's function, as table lamps and candles look wonderful in a living room, yet are somewhat impractical in a kitchen or bathroom.

Deciding upon the position and type of lighting must go hand in hand with deciding upon the position of the furniture. The two are inextricably linked. There is no point planning the ideal place for a reading lamp if there is no chair to go with it, or the best point for a spotlight in a kitchen where there is no work surface.

Once you have worked out your requirements look at the lighting already in the room and note the position of the power outlets. If these are insufficient or simply in the wrong place they must be moved before any other work begins.

▷ **It is much easier to work in an empty room. Make sure any fixtures, such as fireplaces, are carefully covered.**

◁ **Rows of spotlights provide the light required for different functions in this kitchen/dining room.**

surface preparation

"Preparation is all" is a much-quoted and somewhat irritating phrase, but it is nonetheless true. The truth is that however hard you work on a finish it will only be as good as the surface you put it on, and there are few things more disheartening in decorating than having lavished time and effort on a spectacular paint effect, only to have it end up looking disappointingly rough or finding it starts to bubble or flake.

Before starting work on walls, examine them for any signs of damp, crumbling or flaking plaster or cracks. If you discover any of these, then find the cause and cure it, rather than trying to disguise the symptoms you can see.

If the walls have been painted and are in good condition then they need no more than a brush-off then a wash-down with warm water mixed with some dishwashing liquid or mild soap. Once the wall has dried thoroughly, you can hunt out any cracks that need filling. Get as smooth and level a finish as possible, then once dry, sand it. When choosing a filler check that you pick the right one for the job. They range in fineness of finish, from rough exterior grade to very smooth finishes suitable for interior work.

Raw plaster needs to be primed before decorating. Remember that plaster takes a long time to dry out, and even if the surface seems dry, the plaster may well be damp underneath. Fine cracks are also liable to appear as it dries, so decorating too soon can be a mistake. Always use a water-based paint so the wall can breathe.

If the wall has been painted with distemper or textured paint this will have to be

removed before decorating. Wallpaper can most easily be removed with a steam stripper. Many washable wallpapers have vinyl surfaces which you can peel off, leaving a backing resembling lining paper on the wall. This makes a very good surface for painting or wallpapering on to. Alternatively, it can be stripped off.

When working with wood, again look out for any signs of problems, such as dampness, which may cause the wood to warp, crack or crumble.

Painted wood can be sanded and washed down with mild soap, or, if you wish to remove the paint completely, stripped with a chemical stripper or hot-air gun. New wood must first be primed before starting work. Fill holes with a cellulose filler and paint knots with a product such as Bin or Kilz, otherwise they may show through the paint.

using color

Color offers the simplest, cheapest and most effective way of transforming a room. Just by painting the walls, you can totally alter a room's atmosphere.

You can also use color, whether through fabrics, paints or pa to disguise bad features, highlight good ones and even alt proportions. To use color effectively you must first understand its language and characteristics. Different colors have different properties and once you have mastered a few basic rules, you will be able to make colors work to your advantage.

The overall effect of any color will be influenced by other elements, such as lighting, objects in the room (furniture and pictures), as well as the materials, textures and finishes used.

For a basic understanding of how colors work, start by looking at the color wheel. Colors lying on opposite sides of this wheel are called complementary colors – for example, red and green, blue and yellow. These colors have a strong visual resonance so will always work well together, as long as they are used in eq measure and intensity.

Harmonizing colors are those of the same intensity, such as yellow and orange, and these sit together on the color spectrum. Put together they create a very restful atmosphere. Monochrome schemes use various shades of a single color, so tend to be quite muted.

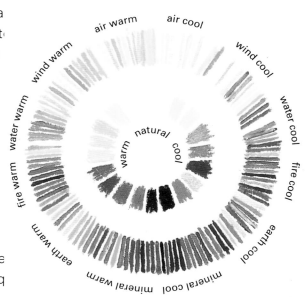

This color wheel is designed to help you choose colors and to discover if you should use warm- or cool-based colors in your home.

effects of color

Learn to distinguish warm from cool colors. Warm colors are based on yellow undertones, while cool colors are based on blue undertones. Any shade of color can have either a warm or cool base, depending on the colors used to make it up. This is especially true of green, which falls in the middle of the color spectrum, halfway between the warm end, consisting of red, orange and yellow, and the cool end, consisting of blue, indigo and violet. This means green can either be made up using warm yellows or cool blues. Rooms painted in warm colors will feel comfortable and welcoming, while cool colors will make a room feel sophisticated and refreshing, yet relaxed.

So it follows that certain colors are more suited to certain rooms with particular functions than others. For example it would not be very sensible to paint a study in too restful a color, while a bedroom painted a vibrant orange will not contribute towards a peaceful night's sleep.

properties of color

While individual colors have their own distinctive characteristics which affect us in different ways, the mass of colors can be divided into light and dark shades, and these can be used to create optical illusions which will alter our perception of space.

Dark shades can be grouped together and described as advancing colors. This is because they make objects painted in those colors appear closer than they actually are. The color brings the object forward. This characteristic can be very useful if you have, for example, a room where the ceiling is disproportionately high for its length

For inspiration and guidance look at how nature mixes colors together.

Simple, wooden decking is given a new lease of life with the use of contrasting blues, enhancing the natural checkerboard design.

Warm shades of orange and blue provide a wonderful backdrop to the rich wood table and striking accessories.

31

The combination of whites and creams accented by a balance of blues makes an unusual, but effective, color scheme for a dining room.

Take pictures of any color combinations that inspire you and keep these for use in future decorating plans.

and breadth. Simply paint the ceiling a dark color and it will appear lower. It is much cheaper than putting in a false ceiling.

Lighter shades work in the opposite way, and so are called receding colors. These can also be used to play visual tricks when decorating, for example, by painting a small room with receding colors you will make it feel more spacious.

Many factors can affect a finished color. For example, colors look different according to the surface on which they are painted. Paint the same color onto a wooden surface and a wall (whether plastered or lined with paper) and the results will be very different, the tone of the color changing according to the surface.

Similarly juxtaposing certain colors can also change their appearance – yellow with white becomes more diffuse, while placed alongside black it seems more intense.

color therapy

Every color has its own particular association that is powerful enough to affect our moods. Just by picturing the color blue you may find yourself thinking of water and the sky. The overall effect is tranquil and fresh, which makes it an excellent choice for living rooms, as well as being a natural choice for bathrooms and kitchens.

Yellow conjures up images of sunshine, making it vibrant and stimulating – a very uplifting color. Orange is also very dynamic and lively, as is its relation, red. Red is vital, and is associated with excitement, while at the same time being extremely inviting and warm.

Green is the color of nature – of grass and leaves. As such it is a color with remarkable calming powers, hence the existence of green rooms in hospitals.

White is a very clean color, and promotes an atmosphere of simplicity and serenity. It can be warm or cool depending on which color dominates the mix used to make it up.

White also has wonderful light-reflective powers, unlike black, which absorbs light. Black needs to be used with care. Too much is oppressive, yet a small amount can look very striking, and combined with colors such as deep reds or purples will look dramatic and opulent.

As a group the neutral colors, soft pastels and whites are naturally soothing. However, the makeup of the color can dramatically change its effect. Cream, for example, may contain yellowy greens, and when choosing a white it is often better to pick one with a hint of another color in it to avoid it looking too clinical.

The shade of the color also has a bearing on how we react to it. In the case of blues and greens, the pale shades, cool watery colors, are wonderfully restful and refreshing, while the darker blues and greens, having more depth, are richer.

inspirational color

When choosing colors, a good starting point is to consider which colors you like the most, and which ones you feel most comfortable with – your instinctive choices. A look around your home will reveal your favorites.

Allow yourself to draw inspiration from any and every source, whether it be nature, a painting, a photograph in a magazine or even a scrap of material. Then think about your furniture, pictures and rugs. Are there any recurring colors you could pick out for the

A rainbow provides the definitive source of color and is a constant source of inspiration.

The classic combination of yellows, whites and greens is a winner for flower arrangements and color plans.

walls and use as the basis of a color plan? After all, unless you have an unlimited budget and can afford to throw away all your furniture and start again from scratch, then the colors should either complement and harmonize in some way, or else provide dramatic contrasts.

Like clothes, colors have their moment of high fashion. This is becoming more pronounced every year as more and more fashion designers branch out into the interior design and paint market, and paint companies follow the decrees of fashion, changing their paint range annually and producing paints which mimic fabrics – such as denim and suede.

While the colors and effects of the moment may be tempting, it is worth remembering that a highly fashionable look may seem dated in a year. A more classic, timeless color scheme has the advantage of lasting for decades and can always be updated with a fashionable accessory.

Colors that hold their charm over time, take inspiration from history. Period houses, whether manor houses or artisans' cottages, can spark off numerous ideas. Many companies now produce their own range of historical paints, so it is easy to reproduce these looks.

Rough walls can be improved by the use of textured paint. This will emphasize the imperfections rather than attempt to hide them.

Think about how one room links through to another. Continuing the signature color in adjoining rooms gives a feeling of unity, but with an individual identity.

combining colors

For any color scheme to succeed you must first decide upon your principal color, which you can use as a signature throughout your house. This signature color can appear as large or small elements in every room, acting as a catalyst to unify and hold the whole look together.

Once you have decided upon your principal color, consider what colors you wish to combine it with. Within any room the colors used can be roughly defined as either base, foreground or accent colors.

The term *base color* refers to the "base note" within a color, in other words the color used as a basis for the paint mix. Two apparently similar colors, for example two greens, may have been mixed using totally different base-note colors – one having a warm base and the other a cool base – and these will determine the ultimate effect the green will have when painted on the wall.

Since the difference between a warm and cool base will have a radical effect on the atmosphere of a room, it is important to get this aspect of color correct before going on to the next stage of picking the foreground colors.

While the background color is the underlying color which will subtly set the tone of the room, foreground colors are the colors that are most immediately obvious as soon as you walk into the room. In other words they are the main colors which appear in the furnishings – curtains and other fabrics, rugs, pictures and furniture. If you wish to engender a feeling of calm and comfort these colors should harmonize with the base color. However, if you are after drama they can contrast.

Lastly, there are the accent colors. These are colors that are used to lift the overall look of the room, either by complementing or contrasting with the base color. They can be introduced in numerous items, such as lamps, cushions, picture frames, and even wall stencils or friezes. When using an accent color it is vital to get the balance correct as an accent color works best in small quantities.

When deciding upon any color scheme, you need to think about more than just one room at a time, because as soon as the connecting doors are opened you will be able to see from one room to another. So beware of color clashes.

Leaves in varying shades of green have been applied to the walls at random. An unusual sink and fixtures give a contemporary look to a country bathroom.

the raw materials

paints and paint products

Until this century the range of paints available was
extremely limited. We now have a huge range
to choose from.

Prior to this century whitewash or lime were
the most common wall treatments. Both are
still available today, and lime wash, in
particular, is well worth experimenting with. It
has a lovely soft, chalky finish and also has the
huge advantage that it allows water to evaporate
through it, making it ideal for old houses where it is
vital that the walls breathe.

Nowadays most people use latex paints for their
walls. These come in various finishes from flat to eggshell
to semigloss to high gloss. Others have either been
designed for a specific area, such as kitchens and
bathrooms, or to produce a particular specialty finish.

There are literally thousands of colors available, ranging from
very brash, bright modern shades to more subtle, traditional
tones. Use paint charts to see how different colors work together.
It is also possible to create your own colors by tinting a base
with poster paints, artists' gouache, acrylics, powder pigments or
universal tints.

For other areas of the house, such as woodwork, oil-based paints are often
used. Among these the best known is gloss, which produces a highly shiny
finish. For a more muted satin sheen, there is eggshell (suitable for walls as
well as woodwork), and finally flat or matt oil. All of these require an oil-based
undercoat. To achieve a rich, high-gloss lacquer enamel is ideal. It can be used
on metal or wood, although is much more expensive and rich than ordinary
gloss, so is best reserved for small areas. Textured paints are useful for
areas which are rough or uneven. They are very thick and can be
difficult to remove when a change of decoration is required.

13 Mineral Gray

16 Terre Vert

14 Verdigris

17 Ultramarine Ashes

5 Invisible Green

18

4 Yellow Drab

7 Bistre

◀ **Look for manufacturers with paint charts specializing in the look you want to achieve and much of the color plan will be done for you.**

Glazes and washes add an extra dimension to a wall or woodwork, giving the color a richness, luminosity and depth not found in a simple flat paint. They can also be used to mimic wood, stone and marble. Three basic types of varnishes are available – gloss, semigloss and matt. All are made from polyurethane, and all produce the same transparent effect, but have different reflective qualitites to create different effects.

A wash consists of nothing more than a thinned water-based paint, while a glaze is basically a medium that can be mixed with paint for a translucent effect. You can brush these over plaster or over a matt base coat.

There are many unusual or specialist paint finishes available. Among these are woodwashes, primers specifically designed to cover ceramic tiles or melamine, acrylic paints, and paints with unusual finishes, such as suede and pearlescent paint.

Traditionally people mixed their own glaze, but it is now available pre-prepared. An oil-based glaze is the best method of achieving broken paint effects such as ragging, dragging and stippling to name but a few. The newer water-based glazes are easier to work with, and are very effective, though not as richly textured as oil-based glazes.

Last but not least, don't forget about using stencils and stamps to create pattern on a surface. These can be used in any room in the house, and can complement both modern and traditional-style interiors. Again, specially formulated products give the amateur decorator the ability to produce professional results.

window treatments

Windows come in every shape and size. There's no limit to what can be done to make windows an interesting and functional focal point in any room.

Windows are enormously important in any room, as they are major focal points and they also allow light and air into the house, while offering the opportunity to look at the world outside – and for the world outside to look in at you. Yet whether your windows are grand or functional, demand to be dressed up or played down, display an amazing view or put you on display to passers-by, they provide an excellent excuse for decoration.

The most popular window dressings are curtains. These provide privacy, keep out the gloom of long winters evenings and the light of too-bright summer mornings and, if heavy enough, provide very effective heat and sound insulation.

They can be made of fabrics, patterns and colors that match or co-ordinate with the rest of the room, or they can be designed to contrast, to provide a touch of drama.

Proportion and scale are just as important as style. Very formal, sumptuous curtains will look out of place at a simple cottage window, dominating the room and blocking out the light. Similarly, short café curtains in rustic homespun cotton would look wrong at gracious floor-to-ceiling Georgian windows, detracting from their stately elegance.

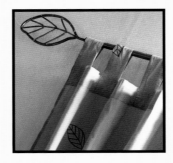

▲ **A contemporary look using tab headings and a decorative rod.**

▲ **Let the light shine in. This bedroom benefits from maximum light with the blinds rolling up from the floor, echoed by plain white bed linen.**

▲ **Long curtains draped behind a rod make an unusual alternative to blinds on attic windows.**

Curtains can be made from almost any type of material, so be imaginative. Indian silk saris come in a myriad of dazzling colors and look spectacular hung as curtains. Similarly, sheer layers of floating muslin look fresh, yet are also practical, both for providing privacy and for insulation – the air trapped between the layers prevents heat loss in winter and will keep a room cooler in summer.

While the most immediate impression comes from the fabric and pattern of the curtains, other details such as the style of valances, fringes and tiebacks make a tremendous contribution to the overall effect.

When deciding on the style of the curtains, consider whether you wish to hang them from a track or a rod. Rods comes in numerous styles and materials, from gilded wood or brass with ornate carved finials, to sleek understated dark wrought iron or copper. If you choose tracks then you may wish to hide them with fabric swags or a valance.

There are many circumstances where curtains are either unsuitable or look wrong. In these cases blinds may be the answer. These come in numerous styles and are made from many different materials. Fabric blinds range from the simplest roller shade – basically a flat, stiffened piece of fabric wrapped around a sprung roller – to the more contemporary Roman blinds and the traditional Austrian and festoon blinds. Blinds can also be made from pleated paper, cane or bamboo. These are cheap and cheerful, so look better in kitchens and bathrooms than in more formal rooms.

Venetian blinds are made from slats hung horizontally and like their cousins, vertical louvres, are made from wood, plastic or metal. Particularly suited to a contemporary setting, they can look extremely chic, and have the bonus that they can be adjusted while lowered to allow in differing amounts of light.

Many older houses have wonderful full-length internal shutters which fold back neatly during the day. These have the advantage not just of covering the window, so keeping prying eyes out and heat in, but of being excellent security.

Shutters can also be external, and in many hot regions they are standard fittings. These can be closed during the hottest part of the day while the window is left open, leaving the room shaded, yet allowing air to circulate.

Shutters work well for large windows.

Try stringing rope through existing Roman blinds to add interest.

wall coverings

Walls are the largest area in any room requiring decoration and the decorative possibilities are enormous, as is the potential impact of your choice.

Wallpapers range from the expensive hand-blocked variety to the mass-produced home center kinds. Many of the mass-produced types are actually made from vinyl or PVC and are washable making them suitable for kitchens and bathrooms. A more attractive, yet also washable, alternative to vinyl is coated wallpaper, which is more expensive but widely available.

Many modern wallpapers are sold pre-pasted, and need only be dipped into a specially shaped water tray before hanging.

There are a huge number of patterned wallpapers, with anything from flowers to geometric shapes on them. Recently, however, many companies have brought out a range of papers designed to emulate decorative paint finishes, such as dragging, stippling or marbling.

Embossed and textured wallpaper can look wonderful in the right circumstances. Anaglypta and Lincrusta have long been popular for the area beneath the chair rail (the area that gets the most wear-and-tear), but they can also look good elsewhere.

Other textured wallpapers include grass cloth, which is often used to disguise rough, cracked walls, and hessian, which was popular in the 1970s, and has become fashionable as a retro look. It is also possible to buy wallpapers which imitate suede, cork, leather and silk. Another well-known textured wallpaper is flock. Real flock is very beautiful and immensely luxurious, and bears little resemblance to cheap flocked wallpaper.

Lining paper makes a lovely soft-looking surface to paint on, as well as hiding minor imperfections in the wall. It also makes an ideal base for expensive wallpaper, creating a smooth, even surface.

You can paste wallpaper borders between the wall and ceiling, or above the chair rail. Besides creating

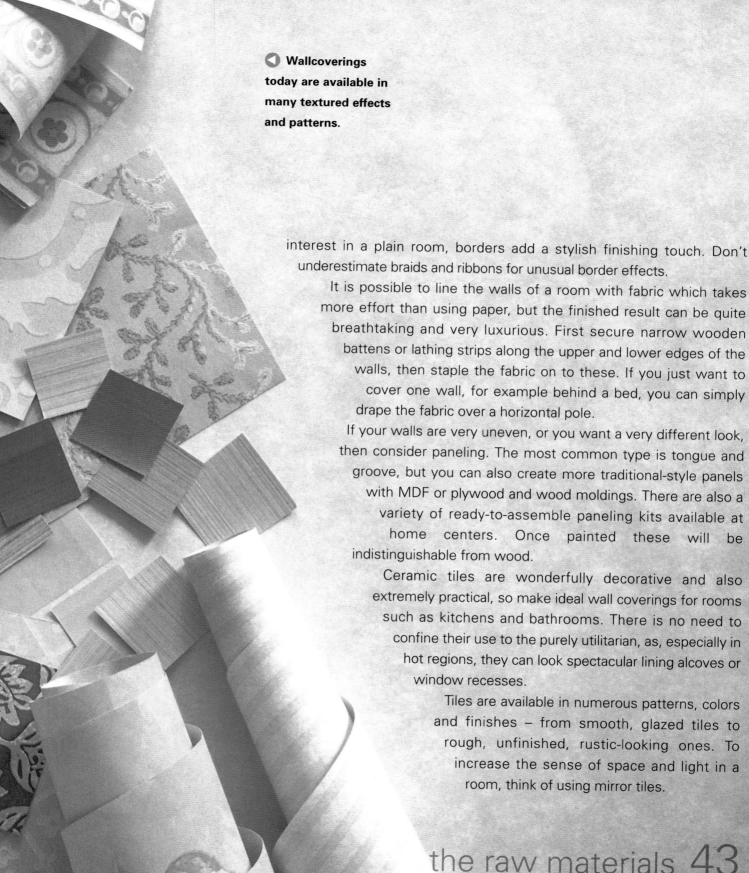

Wallcoverings today are available in many textured effects and patterns.

interest in a plain room, borders add a stylish finishing touch. Don't underestimate braids and ribbons for unusual border effects.

It is possible to line the walls of a room with fabric which takes more effort than using paper, but the finished result can be quite breathtaking and very luxurious. First secure narrow wooden battens or lathing strips along the upper and lower edges of the walls, then staple the fabric on to these. If you just want to cover one wall, for example behind a bed, you can simply drape the fabric over a horizontal pole.

If your walls are very uneven, or you want a very different look, then consider paneling. The most common type is tongue and groove, but you can also create more traditional-style panels with MDF or plywood and wood moldings. There are also a variety of ready-to-assemble paneling kits available at home centers. Once painted these will be indistinguishable from wood.

Ceramic tiles are wonderfully decorative and also extremely practical, so make ideal wall coverings for rooms such as kitchens and bathrooms. There is no need to confine their use to the purely utilitarian, as, especially in hot regions, they can look spectacular lining alcoves or window recesses.

Tiles are available in numerous patterns, colors and finishes – from smooth, glazed tiles to rough, unfinished, rustic-looking ones. To increase the sense of space and light in a room, think of using mirror tiles.

shelving and storage

Every home requires some shelving and storage space, and estimating the amount needed must be one of a decorator's first priorities.

In contemporary houses everything is hidden away behind concealed, streamlined doors. However, maintaining this level of minimalist existence requires such strict discipline that it appeals to relatively few people.

More commonly, people use concealed storage space in bedrooms and bathrooms and practical work areas, such as the study and utility room. Elsewhere it may be acceptable to have more open or semi-open storage in the form of shelves or glass-fronted cupboards.

In the kitchen old-fashioned dressers and plate racks look wonderful groaning with china, managing to combine practicality with beauty. Similarly, racks or bars with butchers' hooks attached to them are excellent for hanging saucepans and utensils, especially stainless steel equipment. Ready-made units offer a wealth of useful storage aids – such as swing-out shelves, bottle and appliance holders and hidden bins – and can easily be adapted to look custom-made. Simply adding some moldings or changing the handles will totally alter their mass-produced appearance.

Built-in cabinets look attractive anywhere. In a bedroom they can be designed to incorporate sliding shelves and racks to hold shoes and ties, drawers specifically designed for underwear, sweaters and T-shirts, as well as the usual hanging space. In bathrooms, cabinets can be built in, under sinks or in the spaces between the bathroom fittings, to hold toiletries as well as towels.

Open shelves have been built on either side and on top of the door, making a wall of practical and attractive storage, suitable for a range of interior styles.

In a very traditional-style house, built-in cupboards and shelves can be disguised using tricks such as covering the doors with fake book spines so that they look as if they are part of a bookcase.

Free-standing bookshelves can look very elegant, while lining the walls of a dull cold room with built-in bookshelves will give it instant character and warmth, the book spines create color, pattern and interest. Free-standing shelves or shelves supported from tensile wires could also be used as room dividers in a contemporary setting.

Cupboards can also be built into alcoves, for example on either side of a fireplace, and deep windows can be given window seats cleverly fitted with lift-up lids hidden under cushions.

△ **Use a window recess to create shelves to show a collection of glass to full advantage, with the light shining through.**

▽ **Wall space in a corridor can be used as a bookcase.**

△ **A cozy chair fits between some unusual and contemporary storage units in a small studio.**

In bedrooms the area under the bed can easily be utilized for storage. Many beds have built-in drawers, otherwise it is possible to buy free-standing drawers which slide out on casters, or else build a custom-made base for the mattress complete with storage space.

Look out for old blanket boxes, ottomans and chests, as these are ideal for storage, as well as being the right height for use as bedside tables.

More contemporary interiors lend themselves to more modern styles, such as modular units, and materials, for example metal or blond woods. There are many industrial shelving and storage units which can be added to or reduced as desired. Many have adjustable shelves which can be moved to suit your changing needs and hold new accessories, such as CD racks.

the raw materials 45

furniture

The style of furniture you choose will be influenced by various factors, such as the period of your home, decorative scheme, budget and practicality.

You will also need to consider new furniture in the context of what you already have and what you wish to keep. Everyone has pieces of furniture that they are attached to – whether it is something that has been passed on down through the family, or something that evokes a particular memory. There is no reason why any decorating scheme cannot accommodate these. There is also no reason why a mixture of styles and periods cannot sit happily side by side – slavish devotion to one period often produces a rather dull scheme and usually dates a home more quickly than a more eclectic approach.

△ **Beds don't need to be on bedframes. Create an Eastern-style bedroom with a rug and dark wood.**

The practicalities of everyday life will determine choice to a large extent, as you will have to consider the wear that furniture and upholstery will be subjected to. A family with small children and pets would be foolish to select furniture upholstered in cream silk. Much better to go for a darker, patterned material treated with a protective coating, and with covers that can be removed for cleaning.

Budget is a large consideration for most people. If the budget is a problem it is worth concentrating on the large pieces vital to any house – such as tables, chairs, sofas and beds – and leaving the extras – such as coffee tables and occasional chairs – to be bought as and when the budget permits.

Look for quality. Buying cheap furniture is often a false economy, as all too soon seats sag, fabrics start to look shabby and chairs become rickety. However, it is possible to pick up pieces in thrift shops which may look tattered, but which can be transformed if painted or reupholstered. If you cannot find the ideal fabric, then a throw draped over a chair or sofa will alter its appearance radically and give an eclectic feel to the room.

△ **Contemporary seating can be a mix of metal frames and fabric cushions.**

◁ **This large upholstered sofa forms the focal point of the room framed by the shelving unit behind.**

▽ **Combine rattan with oak for an updated country look.**

soft furnishing fabrics

Fabrics offer more than comfort; they also provide texture, color and pattern.

Fabrics can also be the unifying force which holds a room together. It is not unusual to find a piece of fabric that you like so much that it not only inspires a whole color scheme, but forms the basis of the decor of a room.

Such a material can be used for more than making curtains; it can transform a selection of cheap or mismatching furniture, giving it a smart unified look.

A table can be made from a circle of plywood set on a stand and dressed up with floor-length circular cloths made from this fabric. Cushion covers can be run up from the same material and it can be used to edge or make lampshades. Even a plain wicker chair can be transformed with a loose cover, slipped over and secured with little fabric ties.

Even if you do not use the same material throughout a room, you can pick out elements of it, such as a particular color, which can provide the linking force in a scheme. By varying the texture and weight of the fabrics used but keeping to this color you will achieve a harmonious but not over fussy look.

The visual appeal of a fabric must be matched by its performance and comfort factor. Fabrics designed for upholstery now have to be treated with a fire-resistant product. There are also many protective treatments which will guard other fabrics against fire, stains and insects, but it is still up to the decorator to choose the right fabric for its intended use. Some need to be more durable than others; for example, the covering of a sofa will get a great deal of wear and must also be comfortable to sit on. So if it is a hot region, a cool, smooth linen will work much better than a warm wool. Think too about using a protective treatment to guard the fabric against stains and general wear-and-tear.

From simple to formal, large to small, fabrics can be found in any design, pattern or plain color. Look out for the new textured finishes and don't forget about trimmings to link a scheme together.

In bedrooms, the linen you choose for the bed is as much a part of the decorative scheme as the curtains or carpets. If you cannot find anything that matches the other colors or patterns in the room, then buy a plain linen in a neutral color and trim it with the same color you have used for the curtains. This will neatly tie it in with the rest of the decor for very little effort and at very little cost.

Alternatively upholster a headboard with matching material, padded with foam, and carry the theme on through with a dust ruffle.

Other treatments which produce a wonderfully luxurious and coordinated look involve using the curtain material to make a canopy for over the bed. This could range from simple folds of fabric suspended from curtain rods above the head of the bed, to a more formal tent effect.

While the kitchen and bathroom require soft furnishings than the rest of the house, there are still many potential uses for fabrics. Windows need to be dressed, shelves can be edged and covers made for any chairs. The bathroom may need a shower curtain, or a curtain to finish off the sink area. The opportunities to use soft furnishings imaginatively are enormous.

Trimmings can be a designer's best friend — they can be used to bring color to a plain curtain or cushions. Patterned furnishings can be finished with a plain-colored edging or border to bring out an accent or dominant color in the design.

lighting

Successful lighting schemes are based on a balance between natural and artificial light, together with the interaction of function and design.

The choice of light fittings available is immense, so much so that the sheer volume of types and styles may prove quite daunting. A good starting point when making a decision is to consider the function the light needs to perform. Is it going to be used to provide background lighting, to create a mood, or is it intended for a more practical purpose – for example, to light a work area in the kitchen.

Generally, lighting can be divided into three main categories: background lighting, such as table lamps, uplighters, and wall and ceiling lights; accent lighting or lights which create a sense of atmosphere, may also illuminate something unusual, interesting or valuable in a room, such as a special picture or piece of attractive porcelain; finally, there is utility or task lighting, where practical considerations are paramount.

These various lighting functions demand different light fittings. Gentle diffuse light may be excellent as background lighting, but is useless, or even dangerous, where food is being prepared and what is needed is a bright light directed at a specific area.

Besides the fitting making a difference to the quality of light, the light source should also be considered carefully. The various light sources commonly used in homes include fluorescent, tungsten halogen, and tungsten. Of these the latter is the most commonly used.

Tungsten bulbs have the advantage of being widely available, cheap and throwing a rather pleasant, warm, yellow light. There are also various tinted bulbs

▲ Modern low-voltage lights suspended on a wire frame 'lower' a high ceiling.

▼ Pools of light from hanging fittings give additional lighting to the cooking area.

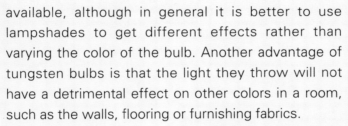

available, although in general it is better to use lampshades to get different effects rather than varying the color of the bulb. Another advantage of tungsten bulbs is that the light they throw will not have a detrimental effect on other colors in a room, such as the walls, flooring or furnishing fabrics.

Halogen bulbs are more expensive than tungsten bulbs, although they should last longer. They throw a much brighter, white light, which has a rather pleasant crispness about it and which will not interfere with other colors. They are particularly effective when used *en masse* and in a modern setting, for example dotted around a kitchen ceiling.

Fluorescent bulbs have improved a great deal over the past few years and do not have such an institutional feel about them any more. While old-style fluorescent tubes had an unpleasant effect on surrounding colors, the newer daylight-simulation types throw a much more sympathetic light. There are also removable covers available which help create a more dramatic effect.

The style of light fitting you choose will depend on the overall look of your room. There are so many different ranges available, from Victorian to minimalist modern, that everyone can find one to suit their needs. Do not be afraid to mix and match – often a minimalist contemporary style will look quite spectacular in an otherwise period room, lifting it from being a traditional style to a vibrant living space.

△ left A combination of table lamps light this dual-purpose room.

△ right High wall lights throw soft light along a corridor.

▽ Lanterns work well in halls and on staircases.

kitchen materials

While many people may be indecisive about how to decorate their homes, when it comes to the kitchen everyone has a strong image of the desired look.

Whatever your taste there are certain practical factors which cannot be ignored. The principle ones are lighting, flooring and work surfaces.

Lighting must be arranged so that work areas are fully illuminated, and the floor should be made of a material that is waterproof, comfortable to stand on for long periods and nonslip.

Work surfaces can be made from natural materials, such as wood, slate or stone, or man-made materials, such as metal, ceramic tiles or plastic laminates. The criteria are that they must be hard-wearing, able to cope with water and heat, and can be easily cleaned.

Wooden work surfaces are very attractive and conjure up comforting images of country kitchens. All kitchen suppliers sell wooden work surfaces and storage units, although for a more individual look it is possible to buy reclaimed timber that can be tailor-made to your requirements. When deciding on a type of wood, bear in mind that the closer-grained varieties, such as beech or maple, are tougher than the softer,

Stainless steel units and appliances create a contemporary look.

A mix of traditional and contemporary with stainless steel and wood.

Painted wooden units update a traditional wooden kitchen.

Smart contemporary laminate units work well with a combination of storage space.

more open-grained woods, such as pine. Wood must be thoroughly oiled or varnished to withstand the constant exposure to water. Wood will also mark if a very hot pan is placed on it, so it is vital to have protective mats or trivets.

Other natural materials, such as granite, marble and slate, also look stunning in a kitchen, and can be designed to appear as traditional or cutting edge as you wish. They require protection against water or heat stains, and should also be guarded against grease, but they will last a lifetime. These materials are also very heavy, a factor which should be taken into account, particularly if the kitchen is not on a ground floor.

Among man-made materials, laminates are probably the most popular in the kitchen. They are cheap and practical, very easy to clean, totally waterproof, and almost completely heat resistant. They are available in many designs, from imitation marble and granite to plain colors – so it is easy to find one to match your planned design.

Stainless steel – the choice of professional cooks – is also immensely practical, being very hygienic, and impervious to water, heat or grease. It's only drawbacks are that it is expensive, will scratch and may appear a little too high-tech for many people's tastes.

Ceramic tiles come in an enormous range of sizes and styles. They are very hard-wearing, although make sure you select heat- and water-resistant tiles for work surfaces. It is also important to choose nonporous, heavy-duty grouting, otherwise it will soon become discolored and unhygienic.

flooring

Unlike other elements in
decorating, such as wallpaper
or paint colors, a floor's primary function is practical.
Whatever surface or covering you choose, it must be able
to withstand the rigors of daily use.

▶ Look beyond
traditional carpets to
discover the innovative
ranges of flooring
available today.

Obviously some areas of the house will take more traffic than others, hallways and corridors being prime examples, while certain rooms, such as kitchens, need floors which can be washed frequently yet will be free from any risk of tripping or slipping.

So the first consideration when choosing flooring must be practical. This will determine whether you choose a soft or hard surface, and whether it should be one which can be easily cleaned. From there you should consider the overall look you are after. The same rules regarding patterns and colors apply as elsewhere in the house, namely that light colors, small patterns and plain surfaces make an area seem larger, while dark colors and busy patterns have the opposite effect.

Flooring materials can be divided into two broad groups: soft and hard. The first category includes carpets, rugs and natural floor coverings, such as coir and sisal, and the hard category contains marble, stone, bricks and similar materials. In addition there is vinyl, wood or cork.

Good-quality carpets can be hard-wearing and they also act as good insulation, in terms of both heat and sound. However, they are more difficult to clean than a hard floor, which can be mopped down, and are not waterproof, so are not good choices for a kitchen or bathroom.

Materials range from pure wool and wool-synthetic mixtures to totally synthetic. How hard-wearing they are is determined by material, density of weave and length of pile. Very dense, short-pile carpets in an 80 percent wool/20 percent synthetic mix are very tough, as are cord carpets, which are made from goat, calf and cow hair woven into a mix of materials. All carpets need a padding or underlay, unless they are foam-backed.

There is an increasing number of totally natural floor coverings available, which look extremely smart while being hard-wearing. These range from

coir and sisal, which although very tough are rather uncomfortable to the touch, to seagrass, jute and rush. Seagrass and rush are less scratchy than coir and are available in very attractive decorative weaves, such as herringbone or plaits. They also come in a range of colors.

Rugs allow you to change the look of a room in an instant, introducing a splash of color or emphasizing colors already present. They can be as plain or decorative, as contemporary or traditional, as you wish.

Many houses have perfectly good floorboards hidden beneath their old carpets. If stripped, sanded and sealed, varnished, painted, dyed or waxed, these boards can look spectacular. If the boards are not in good condition then it is not difficult to lay new ones, or alternatively wood tiles or parquet. The key to a success is to ensure they are laid on a perfectly flat surface.

Other warm yet durable floor surfaces are synthetic vinyl, or natural linoleum, rubber and cork. Vinyl, rubber and linoleum are simple to lay, coming on a roll or as tiles. They are excellent choices for a kitchen, being waterproof and easy to clean. They are also warm, comfortable surfaces to stand on, although rubber scuffs easily. Both vinyl and linoleum are available in every imaginable color and design, even resembling, wood, marble or tiles, while rubber mostly comes in plain colors. Cork comes in the form of tiles, which once laid are sealed to give a warm, semi-soft, nonslip surface. Sealed cork is virtually waterproof, although you can get tiles coated with vinyl which are 100 percent waterproof.

Ceramic tiles make a practical surface, coping well with heavy wear and spills. However, they can be noisy and cold, and are not as comfortable to stand on for long periods as softer, bouncier surfaces.

Marble, stone, slate and terra-cotta look very elegant and luxurious in the right setting. They are particularly suited to hot climates, where they help maintain a cool interior, although they can work well in cooler regions if the rooms are fitted with underfloor heating. They are, however, quite expensive materials and, being heavy, need to be laid on a strong subfloor, which must be completely level.

bathroom materials

Bathrooms are now in a class of their own. Forget the traditional cast-iron tub – look around and discover how innovative you can make your bathroom look.

Water, steam and condensation are constant factors in bathrooms. This must be considered when choosing materials for floors, walls and other surfaces. Good ventilation will help tackle the problems of steam and condensation. However, splashes from the sink and tub are inevitable, especially if there are small children in the family.

Carpets are undoubtedly very warm and comfortable, although it is vital to choose a type made specifically for bathrooms with a waterproof backing. Do not be tempted solely by appearances. Many natural floor coverings, such as seagrass, look stunning but are not practical as they have a tendency to expand and shrink according to how much moisture they absorb. This movement results in nasty gaps around the edges of the room, or wrinkles in the middle.

An alternative to carpet is to lay rugs on top of a more practical floor covering. In this way you will still get the warmth and feeling of luxury a carpet creates, without the water worries – if a rug gets soaked it is a simple matter to pick it up and hang it out to dry.

Vinyl and treated cork make excellent alternatives to carpet. They are practical, being both waterproof and easily washable, and are also warm underfoot. Vinyl is also available in every design and color imaginable, so it is a simple matter to find a style to suit the rest of the bathroom.

Wood looks good in a bathroom, although it is vital to waterproof it, for example with layers of oil-based paint or varnish. Fitting tongue-and-groove paneling is a quick and simple way of creating character while being extremely practical – covering in an instant rough walls and ugly pipework.

⬤ **Traditional tongue-and-groove panels can be used in place of tiles.**

⬤ **Unusual fittings can become the focal point of a minimalist bathroom.**

Double sinks need not be positioned side by side. Think of creating a storage area in-between.

Many materials can be cut to your own design as an unusual backsplash.

Ceramic tiles make excellent wall coverings. In cooler regions all-over tiling can look cold and uninviting, so it is best to restrict them to the areas around the tub, sink and shower.

Walls can also be painted or wallpapered. Most manufacturers produce a range of paints specifically designed for use in the bathroom. These are designed to cope with excess water and to repel mildew, but they only work if the room is well-ventilated. Similarly there are wallpapers available which have been given a waterproof, washable coating, so are impervious to splashes and are easily wiped down.

Fixtures, such as sinks and showers, are usually made from ceramics, plastics or fiberglass. Tubs were formerly made from cast iron and finished with enamel, which is rather cold and very heavy but an attractive look. Nowadays, the majority of bathtubs are made either from acrylic plastic, pressed steel or from fiberglass, and they are available in a broad range of styles that can suit all decorating schemes.

Explore the possibility of glass for sink surrounds and surfaces.

basic decorating equipment

Never skimp on tools. It is a false economy to choose the cheapest – you will find they don't do the job.

There is nothing more infuriating and disruptive than having to pick bristles off paintwork as a cheap brush molts. So invest in the main brands and take care of your tools, cleaning them thoroughly after use, and allowing them to dry completely before putting them away. It is always worth stopping before you get too tired – it's very easy to leave brushes unwashed and find them ruined the next day.

A basic decorating kit should include various items for preparation, such as different grades of sandpaper (from fine to coarse), a variety of scrapers for removing wallpaper and old paint or varnish, mild soap for washing down (rinse thoroughly) and a sander and wallpaper steamer.

Remember that you need to be well protected, especially if you are using chemicals, such as paint strippers, or electrical sanders. Basic requirements are a pair of overalls, a face mask and rubber gloves.

It is worth amassing a good selection of paint containers and trays, as well as some lightweight drop cloths. Light aluminium step ladders are ideal for most home decorating jobs, although a taller ladder may be needed to cope with a high wall, for example on a stairwell. Other necessities are low-tack masking tape or a pieces of stiff card which can be used to prevent paint from spreading where it is not wanted.

There are numerous types of brushes and rollers on the market. Brushes come in a variety of widths, from very fine, narrow brushes for detailed work, to wide heads for larger areas. There are also angled heads for edges and small brushes on long handles for getting at otherwise impossible to reach places, such as behind radiators.

Rollers are useful for painting large areas fast, although they are only suitable for use with water-based paints. Like brushes they come in a variety of widths as well as different textures, ranging from a short to a very shaggy pile. The length of the pile has an effect on the finish you will achieve – a short pile produces a smooth

Try different shaped brushes for unusual paint effects.

Buy everything you need before you start a project and keep it all in one place.

Keep old cans of paint. They can be useful to touch up old paintwork.

finish, while a shaggy pile can be used with textured paints to produce a special effect. These different piles are made to work better on particular surfaces, the short pile being suited to a smooth surface while the long or shaggy pile is designed for a rougher surface.

For wallpapering, besides the steamer and scraper needed to remove old wallpaper, you will need a wallpapering table, bucket and wallpaper paste, a brush with which to apply it, a sponge, sharp scissors and craft knife, a pencil, tape measure, and plumb line to check that you are hanging the sheets straight.

Finally, after all the preparation and after you have completed the job itself, you will need to clean up. Some paints, such as latex, are water-based, so brushes and rollers can simply be cleaned with water. Oil-based paints, however, are harder to clean, and require solvents, such as white spirit or turpentine, to remove all traces.

interior design masterclass

introduction

So far, this book has covered the basic principles required and the raw materials you need for successful interior design. These masterclasses will now teach you how to work with individual rooms in the home. Each masterclass is divided into eight parts which are the key areas to consider when designing a room.

principles

Each room has its own set of rules, but there are also some basic principles that can be applied to every room. Start by looking at the proportions of the room and noting any architectural features. Understand the structure of the room and note what its main use is. If it is possible to reposition a misplaced fixture, the money spent will be well invested.

lighting

Lighting presents one of the most exciting challenges when designing a room, and the choices are infinite. As a general rule, I prefer to use overhead lighting in "functional" areas and low-level lighting in "living" rooms. In the masterclasses, I explain how different light sources can create different effects, and suit the usage of each room.

floors

A floor can alter the entire look of a room, so it is vital to get this right before you make decisions on other areas. I like to use the same flooring throughout all the main rooms, using a neutral carpet or a natural floor covering like sisal or seagrass, but you may feel that you wish to address specific requirements. Getting the look you want need not be expensive, with old wooden floors and new vinyls being versatile and very popular.

color plan

Think about color throughout the room, not just on the walls. If in doubt, keep your color plan simple – it can be better to use several shades of the same color, rather than clutter a space with too many colors. Also, think about painting your woodwork in a dark color. Baseboards look wonderful in shades of gray or taupe, particularly with pale walls. One of

🔺 **A plain roller blind has been painted to co-ordinate with the fabric.**

🔺 **A modern picture works with an antique fireplace and plain walls.**

A circular table top can hide a multitude of sins. Here, a filing cabinet is hidden under the cloth.

my favorite tricks is that I rarely use pure white paint. All my ceilings and woodwork are generally painted in a "soft" white. Once the room is completed and furnished it will look white and acts as a hidden catalyst to link colors.

design theme

Broadly speaking design themes can be separated as follows: traditional/contemporary; country/city; formal/informal. Be brave and mix your styles. Modern paintings can look wonderful in an updated traditional room. Equally, a faded, old-fashioned floral design can work well in a contemporary setting. The secret is to make sure there at least two items of a similar period to create balance. I always prefer to work to a "theme" rather than a "set" style. A rigid, set style can look very contrived, and I prefer to aim for a more eclectic individual design theme.

furnishings

Take time buying furniture and soft furnishings. You can make expensive mistakes in a rush to complete a room. Always make sure that any arrangement of furniture is balanced. One trick is to ensure that a piece of furniture always has something to "talk" to. A chair on its own in a living room will look very isolated, but placed next to a side table or another chair, it will become part of the room. If you want to use a range of patterned fabrics, use the largest design on the largest area, for example in the curtains, a mid-size pattern for a sofa or tablecloth, and the small designs for cushions and accessories.

details

Details, although usually small items or accents, are the hidden link to bring your decorating scheme together. It could be an accessory or the repetition of a particular fabric that can really make the room feel like home. On this spread you can see how I have used a fabric in a room in my present house. This fabric has moved with us from two previous houses, and is the detail that has linked our homes together.

final touch

I have also included suggestions that will provide the finishing touch to your room. This is often fragrance, in the form of aromatic candles, bowls of lavender, herbs and spices or fresh flowers. It could also be a special painting or a quirky conversation piece.

hall

From the moment you walk through a front door, it is the hall that gives you an insight into what you will find beyond. First impressions count, and although a hall is often perceived as just a passageway, it is one of the most important rooms in the home.

principles

A hall is principally used as a route to get from one room to another. Rarely is there the luxury of being able to use the hall as a room to live in. Think laterally about the space, and look at the rooms that lead off the hall. Could a wall be knocked down to include the hall space in another room? Remember to check with local building regulations before making any structural changes.

Work out if there is room for a telephone table, or wall space for coat hooks or for a coat closet. Chairs give a lived-in feeling to the room and are also welcoming for visitors. Even in a narrow hallway, try to have a shelf for keys and letters to avoid having them left on the floor or on surfaces you intend for ornaments.

● **Knocking down the wall between a narrow hall and the room next door has created a large and light hall with additional living space.**

▼ **A carpet runner links the carpets used on the ground and upper floors.**

lighting

Hall lighting has two functions. First, bear in mind safety; an entrance and staircase must be well lit. Second, think about how combined use of different lighting and dimmers can add a welcoming, relaxed atmosphere, especially if the hall leads straight into the living room.

Generally halls have overhead lighting. If your hall has a single pendant light, think about moving it and adding another light. A single light can make the space look smaller, whereas two lights placed farther apart gives the illusion of a larger area. Combining ceiling lighting with wall lights (on separate switches) is very effective, especially on long, narrow hallways where there is no natural light.

floors

Hall flooring has to be practical and hard-wearing. Steer clear of pale colors, which will be difficult to maintain. If you do move to a house that already has a pale carpet that you cannot justify replacing, inexpensive rugs can protect the areas of hardest wear and contribute to the overall color scheme. Doormats are essential for all entrance halls. Rather than a loose mat, think about cutting a mat well into the floor, and using a colored coir mat, thereby creating a functional as well as unusual design feature. Hard flooring is ideal for halls, and there is a huge choice of materials available to suit the style of your property.

color plan

The color plan in a hall should always relate to and link together the colors used throughout the house. Particular attention should be paid to how you link colors, pattern and texture in hallways. The colors used in the hall should establish the "signature" color for the house if you are going for a harmonious theme. Paint effects can be particularly effective. Alternatively, if you decorate with bold contrasting colors, patterns achieved with wallpaper or paint techniques such as stenciling or stamping can bring all the colors together.

design theme

Following the guidelines outlined for colors, bear in mind the same thoughts when thinking about the design themes. The hall should "set the scene" for the overall style of the house, although different rooms can reflect a variety of themes. You could have a contemporary kitchen with a traditional Victorian living room for instance, and your hallway could help to link them together. Often an eclectic theme works well in a hall, combining ancient with modern and reflecting individuality. Anything that can make a hall appear welcoming will work well – perhaps photographs or paintings of favorite places or holidays? A child's painting well-framed can be very stylish and fun.

furnishings

Hall furniture should be practical, but quirky unusual designs can give the room character. Halls can have awkward proportions so always keep a lookout for unusual pieces that could fill a space too small or narrow for standard furniture. Basic storage will help keep the hallway clutter-free, so look at the available space objectively, and see if there is anywhere you could build a bookcase, put a desk or create storage under the stairs.

Few soft furnishings are generally required in hallways, unless the room has a dual purpose, but full-length curtains over the front door can be very effective for keeping out drafts in winter and blinds over windows can keep the hall cool in summer.

details

Go to town on decorative accents and details in a hall. Small spaces and minimal use of furniture mean you can use details to their best advantage, but do not be tempted to clutter the space. "Less is more" could have been written with halls in mind! A single picture can be more effective than lots of little "postage stamps" on the walls.

final touch

To complete the picture, a scented candle in a hall is a must. There is a multitude of choice now available and any mood can be created. Nothing is more inviting than a delicious scent when entering a home, and this can make you never want to leave.

◐ **Panels give the room architectural proportion, balanced by the chairs either side of the fireplace.**

◑ **Valances are used to disguise windows of different heights. The recess provides additional seating.**

kitchen

My kitchen combines a country theme with Shaker-style simplicity.

A wooden plate rack above the sink is both decorative and functional.

Mix and match cushions in the same design, but in different colors.

For many a kitchen is the heart of the home. Some may only pop into the kitchen to make coffee, but for many it is the room they may spend quite a lot of the day in, either preparing, cooking or eating food and spending time with the family.

principles

Kitchen design is based on four basic principles: storage, preparation, cooking and eating. The design of any kitchen, no matter how large or small, has to take all these factors into account, and provide logically designed space for each function.

Kitchen layouts are divided principally into six categories: U-shape, L-shape, double galley, single galley, peninsula, and island. Kitchens can be designed from one or a combination of these layouts depending on the size or shape of the room.

lighting

Ceiling spotlights placed over working areas and throughout the room are essential for a well-designed kitchen. Under-wall unit lights are a useful bonus, especially in a kitchen that you eat in. The strong overhead lights can be dimmed or turned off. You can then dine by candlelight, supplemented by a subtle light source from around the perimeter of the room.

floors

Kitchens can have any floor surface that can be easily cleaned. Base your choice on what suits the size and style of your room. Wood suits many kitchen styles, but can be expensive to install and maintain. The range of sheet vinyl made today is infinite. No longer the clinical vinyl of the past, it is available at all prices and in a range of finishes that imitate woodgrain, marble, metal and tiles. Ceramic tiles are an obvious choice for kitchens; both practical and hard-wearing, they work well in many decorating schemes. Carpet is unwise as spills will ruin most carpets. Carpet tiles are an option as it is easier and cheaper to replace just one or two as they become worn.

color plan

No color plans can start before you have chosen your kitchen units. Once the choice has been made, you can then start thinking about the colors you would like to use. Next, think about the wall tiles; more often than not it is the choice of tiles dictates which colors will be selected.

◀ **Inspiration for our kitchen color plan was taken from these blue, white and yellow door panels.**

▶ **Yellow walls, off-white units, blue accessories and a blue-and-white check blind link the colors together. A merchant's chest provides ample drawer space.**

design theme

Take your lead from the style of units and choice of tiles, as they are the most expensive and permanent parts of a kitchen. A design theme could be inspired by a family collection of hobbies, the design chosen for the blinds, or a favorite piece of ceramic. Keep the theme simple since a kitchen is full of essential equipment and accessories.

furnishings

Most kitchen furniture will be built in, leaving space for only a table and chairs in a combined kitchen and dining room, and probably only a stool in a small room. Large kitchens where space isn't at such a premium can take an unfitted look. A design scheme based around individual pieces of furniture gives you the freedom to create your own look. Use window treatments to bring some pattern into the room. These can be checks or stripes for a minimal look or a floral design for a more traditional room.

Look at the space leading off your kitchen as often there is more than a door into a kitchen and there can be spare space that can be turned into a cupboard. Top of the list must be kitchens large enough to have a separate seating area, which turns the kitchen into another living area in the home.

details

Go shopping and look for basic kitchen utensils and other items to coordinate with your color scheme. A small picture or a decorative ornament can make a kitchen appear less functional. You could also update inexpensive hardware such as your kettle or toaster.

final touch

Herbs growing on a windowsill in appropriate containers bring an herb garden into your kitchen.

small kitchen

Designing a small kitchen is an interesting challenge, and requires a great deal of ingenuity to fit everything in. Once completed, though, the result is a totally practical functional area that is often easier to use than a large kitchen.

principles

Think very carefully about everything you are going to need. Cast away anything that is not vital or used every day. Small kitchens are often "gallery-shaped," with everything arranged and stored in a long line. The oven often works best in the center with the sink on one side and the preparation area on the other side. Check before you start that all the required services (water, gas and electric outlets) are in place. Also check any building regulations.

◀ Tall units at either end of this galley-style kitchen create additional storage. Granite is used both as a backsplash and as a worktop.

▼ A stainless steel oven matches the steel units.

lighting

The lighting in small kitchens has to be focused. Careful placing of ceiling spotlights can make the space seem larger. A square arrangement of recessed spotlights could make a narrow kitchen look wider for instance. Under-wall unit lighting aids preparation work, and a light over the stove can be useful too.

floors

Floors in small kitchens are subject to a lot of wear-and-tear over the same area. Wooden floors will soon show wear in a particular patch usually near the sink and oven. Heavy-duty vinyl or ceramic tiles make the best choice, as they are easy to maintain and ceramic tiles rarely show signs of wear.

color plan

Keep to a disciplined color plan in a small kitchen. The more colors you use the smaller it will look. Think about using metallic units and glass cupboard doors which act like a mirror to reflect the light. Strong use of white also adds to the illusion of space.

design theme

Small kitchens benefit from simple design themes. With a small kitchen, especially galley shape, you are looking at a rectangular space which will require careful planning. Small kitchens tend to be in apartments converted from houses, or in loft apartments, and you should try to follow the style of property. Traditional themes could follow a simple Shaker style. High-tech kitchens can make the best use of contemporary materials.

furnishings

Tiles rarely work in small kitchens. The line separating the worktop from the tiles will make the space seem smaller. Instead, think of continuing the worktop material up on the wall to the base of the wall units. No matter what material is chosen, the overall effect expands the space, making it look both taller and wider. Small kitchens rarely have space for any furniture. A shelf on hinges can be used as a drop-down table. Any spare space under a worktop can store a stool or you could choose a fold-up chair that can be tucked behind a door.

details

Details are a luxury small kitchens can rarely afford. If your room can spare the space, a bowl of fruit is both useful and will give color accents to the disciplined design scheme.

final touch

A contemporary bulletin board will help you stay organized.

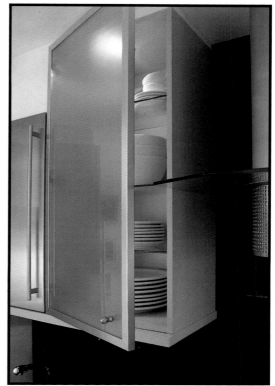

Illuminated
glass doors break
up the solid line
of wall units and
reflect light.

White walls,
floors and
woodwork contrast
with the black and
steel to create the
illusion of a much
larger space.

dining room

Dining rooms are an asset to any home, and the bonus of having a separate room to eat in is hard to beat, especially if you have a small kitchen. Careful attention must be paid when planning a dining room – there's a lot more involved than just buying a table and chairs!

principles

Check that you have enough space to use a room as a dining room. As a rough guide, allow 12–16 sq. m/14–19 sq. yds to seat six people comfortably. Think about how you are going to use the room. Will it be dedicated to entertaining on an occasional basis, or will it be used by the family for all meals? Do you want to create a formal or informal room? Will the room double up as a workspace or study? All these considerations need to be balanced and taken into account.

lighting

Dining rooms must have lighting that is both atmospheric and practical. Lights connected to individual switches and dimmers are an effective means of achieving different lighting effects. A good starting point is to install a pendant light in the center of the table. This casts a relatively large area of light over a focused point. If you have an adjustable fitting, this can be lowered for a more intimate effect if there are fewer people.

Work out where light is needed in other parts of the room. If you have a large dining room, it will require additional ceiling lighting, and remember to provide lighting for any furniture, especially if it is used for serving food. You could also plan to supplement lighting with candles.

inset **Plain china and cutlery suit a simple design.**

A Swedish-inspired theme based on blue.

A crystal sconce is typical of Swedish design.

floors

Carpets are a good solution for dining room floors as they act as good sound mufflers. Unless you have a very modern design theme, vinyl tends to look very clinical. However, with the current move toward natural floor coverings and wood, these should also be considered. The neutral tones of natural floor coverings enhance any decorating scheme, traditional or contemporary. Their construction makes them the ideal solution if you want to use soft colors that are hard-wearing and don't show every speck of dirt or dropped food. Over a period of time though, the movement of chairs will start to show on any flooring surface. One of the main advantages of a wooden floor is that it can be sanded to remove any marks, and then repainted, stained or varnished.

color plan

Dining rooms can be calm or dramatic, depending on the use of the room. Pale, cool shades such as these blues are ideal for a room that is used by all the family and doubles up as a workspace. As long as you use a tone that has some depth of color you will notice that it reflects different shades according to the time of day.

Alternatively, be bold! Deep or bright colors can be used to great effect in dining rooms. It's said that these colors stimulate the appetite and encourage lively conversation, they're thus ideal for entertaining and for rooms used mainly in the evening.

design theme

Choose a theme that complements the use of the room. A family dining room that doubles up as a room for entertaining would benefit from simple decoration that can be altered with accessories. If the dining room connects directly to another room, ensure the individual room themes

△ **Painted furniture is an essential element of Swedish design.**

◁ **Striped dress curtains are used with a simple blind and a decorative painted valance.**

▷ **Bring life to old chairs by making covers to match the curtains.**

work together. Inspiration can also be taken from pictures, fabrics and your china design.

furnishings

Dining room furniture usually consists of the basic table and chairs, and a side table if space permits. Any additional wall space could be used for spare chairs and storage. Do make sure that there is enough space for people to circulate. Nothing is worse than spilt soup when someone is trying to squeeze past! Give some thought to the table shape. A square or octagonal table makes an innovative change from traditional circular and rectangular tables. Seating should always be comfortable, and the style should reflect the amount of use it will get. Large rooms can take curtains, but it is better to use blinds in small rooms, so the space is not minimized. Make use of tablecloths since they not only act as a protection for the surface below, but are an easy and inexpensive way to add to the overall theme.

▲ **A collection of blown eggs contribute to a natural style.**

details

Pay as much attention to your table settings as to the actual decoration itself. Try to have china that complements your color plan. When entertaining, little touches such as carefully chosen napkin rings and candlesticks add interest and diversity to an occasion. Choose pictures that encourage conversation and work with your color scheme.

final touch

Dining rooms that are not used every day can look cold and unused. Try keeping a bowl of pot pourri or fresh flowers in the room, so the room feels lived in at all times.

living room

Living rooms are no longer perceived as traditional drawing rooms. Instead we now have rooms that are truly "lived" in – a place that combines family rest and play, together with the pleasure of entertaining guests.

principles

Seating is the focal point of a living room, although the position of a table and chairs will also have to be taken into account if the room doubles up as a dining room. When planning, allow 30 cm/ 12 in between upholstery and tables, a minimum of 60 cm/24 in to walk between any seating, free-standing furniture and doors. A living room needs a focal point around which to base your design. This is generally a fireplace but for living rooms without a fireplace, it could be based around the seating arrangements, with a coffee table as the focal point in the center.

lighting

Low-level lighting is less harsh than lights placed overhead. Living rooms benefit from table lamps to give both ambient lighting and a focused directional light source for reading. However, large rooms and contemporary design themes will also benefit from strategically placed spotlights, especially useful for lighting pictures. Lights that point up can create dramatic light effects, especially with contemporary design schemes. Different lighting levels can be used to create a variety of moods depending on the use of the room at any one time.

A stunning contemporary look is created using white with strong, contrasting colors.

floors

Just about anything goes for living room floors. Wooden floors, either plain, stained or wood-washed, can be equally effective as carpeting. The choice of flooring will largely depend on the room's principal use, but your choice will also be influenced by your style of decoration. Traditional themes sit well with carpets, although having a wooden floor is a simple way to give traditional furnishings a different contemporary look. Modern themes look great with pale, bleached wooden floors, which can be given some color by the addition of a rug.

color plan

As a general rule, dark colors used in living rooms tend to look traditional and brighter colors reflect a more contemporary look. However, rules are made to be broken, and you should choose a color scheme that suits the way you live. Don't be tempted to use too many colors. Living rooms have a more diverse selection of furniture than any other room in the house. Upholstery reflects large blocks of color or pattern, and you should ensure that the colors, patterns and textures you use are evenly balanced throughout the room.

design theme

When considering how to decorate your living room, it is worth bearing in mind the architectural style of the house. Although you can mix different themes within your home, the living room is probably the first room you and any guests will walk into after the hall, and it is well worth thinking

▶ **The white walls are given a modern look with painted stripes in mauve, yellow and green.**

▼ **The stripes are picked up in the cushion fabric.**

Carefully chosen accessories pick up the stripes. This elegant vase echoes the linear wall design.

about taking the inspiration for your design theme from the house itself. Successful design themes can also be based on an individual rug or picture, echoing the design and colors of everything throughout the room.

furnishings

Seating is your priority, and do make sure that you buy comfortable upholstery, with good-quality cushions that will last. Living rooms often have a variety of seating, moving on from the traditional matching three-piece suites. Not only does this give an eclectic feel to the room, but it gives you the opportunity to experiment with different fabric textures and designs. It usually works better to place contemporary furniture in a room with traditional architectural features, than to put traditional furnishings in a modern loft apartment.

details

Mix old with the new, but not too much! An old piece of china can look wonderful with a contemporary glass vase. Although one can be patterned and the other plain, make sure there is a common color to link the two together. Living rooms can have a lot of wall space. Combine a large painting on one wall with four small ones arranged to look like one large picture hung on the opposite wall. Pictures of a similar size but of various subjects can be reframed with matching or tonal picture mounts, to create an interesting and eclectic collection of pictures that do not look out of place together.

Reframe your pictures to work with a new design scheme. Again, glass echoes the green elsewhere in the room.

Well-chosen accessories such as this writing box and vase complete the look.

final touch

Personal craft items can add interest to a living room. A tapestry, painting or drawing that a member of the family has produced can look wonderful when framed well. You could also think about commissioning your own painting to suit the style of your living room.

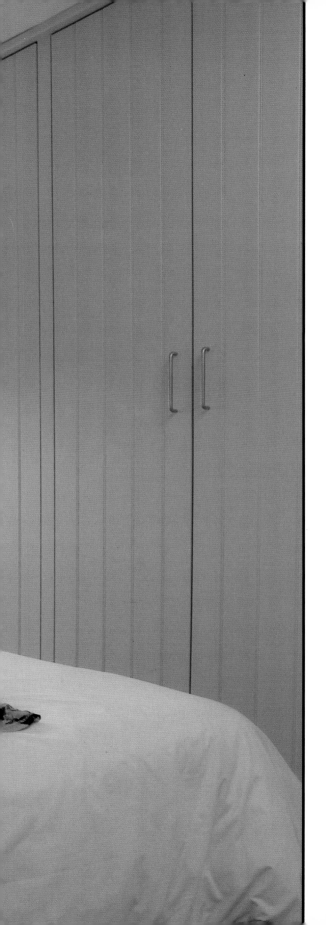

bedroom

A bedroom can be just somewhere to sleep or a sanctuary for relaxation. We spend more time here than any other room in the house, but most of it tends to be when we are asleep.

principles

Most people dream of having a large bedroom, but in reality a small room can be more intimate and just as practical. The essentials are to plan where the furniture will fit and check that you have enough room for storage. If you are planning your own room and are short of closets, think of making closets in landing recesses, or using closets in a guest room. The bed is the focal point in any bedroom, and as a basic guide, you should always allow 75 cm/3 ft around the bed for circulation. Next on the list is to make sure you have invested in a comfortable bed. It is better to wait to decorate your room than skimp on a cheap bed. Then look outside your window – do you live on a noisy street? If so, think about investing in some double-glazing units for the windows to ensure a good night's sleep – this has the additional bonus of providing heat insulation during the winter months.

Paint accessories in colors to match the room.

Greens and blues combine to create a modern and tranquil room.

lighting

Soft, subtle lighting works best in bedrooms. Ideally low-level lighting is best, which can be complemented by soft-colored light bulbs. If you already have a central pendant fitting, keep it and make it a decorative feature. The removal of a ceiling fixture inevitably leaves a mark, which can be particularly annoying to look at when lying in bed! If a hanging light would look out of place, (after having moved a bed, for example), think about replacing it with a recessed spotlight which can be angled away from the bed to light a picture on the opposite wall. Make sure you can switch the lights off from your bed. Individual dimmers on table lights can be a blessing when a partner wants to read and you are trying to sleep.

floors

Bare feet walk across bedroom floors! Wooden floors are very popular and reflect the mood of today's decorating themes, but carpets are softer to walk on. The bedroom is one place where you can have pale-colored carpets without the fear of constant marks from the dirt outside.

color plan

Bedrooms are places of relaxation, which benefit from the use of soft and pale colors. Greens and blues, pinks and peaches, all work well. Bold colors stimulate rather than relax the brain, but owners of brightly colored bedrooms say that it makes getting up in the morning easier! Bedrooms decorated using different shades of the same color can be the solution to the balance between pale and bright colors, but don't be tempted to use too many shades! As a rule three to four shades work the best. Choosing the colors from the same paint manufacturer ensures you will get an even balance of color.

design theme

Popular bedroom designs reflect floral images. The garden is perceived as an oasis of calm and a place of rest, which probably explains why these designs are often used in bedroom

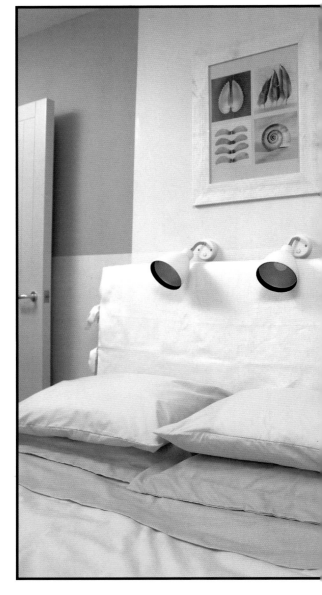

The wall behind the bed is painted with squares imitating the blind design.

Natural wool carpet is ideal for bedrooms.

The geometric blind pattern echoes the aqua shades with accents of beige and white.

Contemporary frosted glass accessories are accented by a simple chrome photo frame.

furnishings. Traditionally, floral designs were perceived as being old-fashioned (cabbage roses, for example). Recently, the contemporary floral design has taken off and any pattern can be created using flowers as your inspiration. With the bed as the focal point, the design theme can also be taken from your choice of bedlinen. Try basing your decoration around a duvet cover design. Alternatively, if you have large windows in your room, use a patterned fabric for your window treatment and pick up the colors in your choice of bedlinen.

furnishings

Bedlinen will be the principle source of furnishings in your bedroom. This will be complemented by your choice of curtains or blinds. Traditionally, bedrooms always had curtains, principally to keep out the light at night, but also to keep the room warmer in cold climates and cooler in hot parts of the world. Nowadays, with the advent of specialty blinds, the choice of window treatments is infinite. Do you have a small bedroom? If so think of using blinds which will create the feeling of more space in the room. Ensure you have somewhere by your bed for at least a lamp and a clock. If space is at a premium, think of using wall lights and a shelf fixed to the wall to act as a bedside table.

detail

Do not be tempted to clutter your bedroom with too many accessories. Photographs add a personal touch and pictures representing favorite places can look good on the walls and mean you can lie back in bed and think back over wonderful trips or places you dream of going to.

final touch

Spray some of your favorite scent in the room while you are getting ready for bed.

child's
bedroom

Do you remember your bedroom as a child? Your first impressions of life are largely formed from what you see around you. A bedroom is the central point of a child's life, and its memories can endure forever.

principles

Throughout childhood, a child may live in the same room, either alone, or sharing with a brother or sister. Plan their rooms from the start with flexibility in mind. Much will depend on whether the child uses the room as a playroom as well as a bedroom.

Safety considerations are a priority. Fit window locks and door gates when your child is a baby, and easy-to-use door handles for when they get older. Provide nightlights to light the way to the bathroom.

lighting

Safety plays a big part here in a child's room and there should be overhead lighting until children reach school age. Ensure that you have provided outlets for computers and stereos for when they are older. These must be covered with socket covers when they are babies or toddlers. Dimmer switches can be particularly useful when changing babies' diapers or tending to sick children during the night. Teenagers will love them later on to create interesting lighting effects.

floors

Children's floors must be practical and hard-wearing. Cork or cushioned vinyl is ideal if the room doubles up as a playroom (train sets don't run well on carpet). If the room is mainly a bedroom, carpet is the better option. Cord carpets are particularly hard-wearing and mid-dark colors do not show every speck of dirt. Rugs help protect the carpet, and are easy to change as the child grows up.

color plan

It is said that babies and children respond best to bright colors. Primary colors are certainly popular for babies, but as children get older, you can maintain the bright color theme, but with more exciting combinations of colors. Some people prefer pale, restful colors for babies. There are no set rules. Yellow is a popular color for babies' rooms; it covers all eventualities if you do

not know if you are expecting a boy or a girl! In any case, with such a large choice of children's furnishings available, the old rules of blue for a boy and pink for a girl need no longer apply.

◀ **Think about every detail. Here, snake drawer knobs complete the look.**

◢ **Brightly colored murals of animals decorate the walls.**

design theme

Don't take the decoration of a child's room too seriously! It is their room, and children see life in a different perspective from adults. Try to let children express what they would like in their rooms from an early age. It is all part of the formation of character, and will reflect their interests and hobbies as they grow up. You can go to town and create a "fantasy world" for a child to live in. Another

▷ **Even unused fireplaces can be put to use as a child-height bulletin board.**

solution is to keep the basic room decoration plain and simple. Inevitably there is always a current fad, be it Barbie or Star Wars. However, if the room is simply decorated, a duvet cover or poster from the current trend will satisfy the child's interest, and is inexpensively replaced when the next craze looms on the horizon.

furnishings

Children's furnishings should always be functional, practical and washable. Sticky fingers and wandering pens can enhance or create a design on every child's fabrics and walls! (Wallpapers are to be avoided; washable wallpaper borders are very effective.) Paint effects work very well in children's rooms as they are easy to apply, and the textured finish hides the odd mark (or two or three!). Try using two colors applied individually to get an interesting contrasting or tonal effect. Think through what you have to store in the room. There will be toys as well as clothes, especially if it doubles up as a playroom. When looking for furniture, look at the collections designed especially for children. You can be sure they are safe and practical, and most are designed to adapt to the changing needs of children as they grow up.

details

A bulletin board is a must in a child's room. It can serve as an art gallery for small children's artwork and then can progress to a place to keep schedules and essential information for school children. Use posters for pictures. Applied to the wall with pushpins or low-tack tape, they can easily be removed when different images are required.

final touch

The ceiling painted sky-blue, with self-adhesive fluorescent planets, moon and stars, will ensure that your child truly lives in a world of his or her own.

en suite bathroom

Never underestimate what you can fit in a small space. Even the smallest room can be made into a bathroom. People often think that limited space can take only a shower unit but this can sometimes be a problem with low ceilings. Skillful use of space, combined with smaller fixtures can result in the addition of a room you may not have thought possible.

principles

Plans for new bathrooms must always be checked with the relevant authorities. Think about how you can use every available space and try not to think of it as you would a main bathroom. Don't think that you always have to include a toilet; you could be trying to include too much in one space. Oval baths are worth investigating as they can increase the illusion of space.

lighting

If you do not have any natural light, ensure you have planned enough sources of artificial light. Low-voltage ceiling lights are much smaller than conventional fittings and small spotlights are ideal for low ceilings.

floors

Opinions differ as to the suitability of carpets for bathrooms. Personally, I have never needed to replace a carpet used in a bathroom. If a bathroom is *en suite* from a carpeted bedroom, I suggest you continue the same carpet into the *en suite* to make the room appear larger.

color plans

Small bathrooms will benefit from a link to the colors used in an adjacent area. With *en suite* bathrooms, look at the bedroom decoration and think how you can vary the use of the bedroom colors to give the bathroom individual but related color themes.

design themes

Large patterns should not be restricted just to large rooms. Often the use of an overscale pattern can "explode" the space around it, thereby making the space seem larger. Check that your wallpaper is suitable for bathrooms or apply a coat of special varnish to protect the surface from steam and condensation.

furnishings

There will be little room for furnishings in a small bathroom. Cabinets will dominate a room, and make it seem even smaller. An alternative is to create a fabric skirt around a pedestal sink. This softer decorative treatment is an inexpensive and effective means of including a soft furnishing element and you can use the space underneath for storage. Keep any tiles simple; a plain color that blends with the walls will expand the width of the room and give the illusion of a higher ceiling.

details

In a small area, nothing goes unnoticed. Because of this, hide any pipes behind false walls or you will find your eye drawn to them. Again, "less is more," so do not clutter up any surfaces with unnecessary objects. Concentrate your efforts on beautiful essentials such as faucets and light switchplates.

final touch

Buying bath essences in colors that coordinate with the overall color scheme completes the picture.

inset Fittings placed in the center of the bath make the room appear larger.

This bathroom was created from a walk-in closet.

The wallpaper in the bathroom matches the bedroom curtains. The curtain fabric has been used to make a storage area under the sink.

bathroom

Bathrooms and shower rooms are often perceived as functional, uninviting rooms. In reality, they can be havens of calm and tranquility where you can escape the stresses of everyday life.

principles

Essential bathroom fixtures and equipment have to take priority when planning a bathroom. If you are designing a room from scratch, play around with all the different ways your basic fixtures might fit into the space. Ensure there is adequate ventilation (check building regulations). If you have the luxury of being able to fit both a shower unit and bathtub in the same room, seek expert advice to ensure your boiler can provide enough hot water.

inset **The room colors are echoed in the glass table.**

Wood cut in a wavy pattern is an alternative to traditional wall tiles.

lighting

The main consideration with lighting in a bathroom is safety. The fitting you choose must be sealed against water penetration and condensation. Spotlights positioned above sinks and mirrors are very useful.

floors

Bathroom floors must be made from nonslip materials. A wood floor must be well sanded and varnished to protect feet. Vinyl can create a futuristic look, or it can be covered with a rug that can double up as a bath mat. Bath mats usually have nonslip bases, but if you use a rug, place a nonslip liner underneath for additional safety. Ceramic floor tiles can be slippery, but coordinating floor and wall tiles can make a stunning design scheme.

Curved shower doors continue the wave theme, and inexpensive tiles continue the color.

Green decor and white bathroom fittings are linked together with striped curtains.

color plans

Think of your favorite color and use it! All colors work in bathrooms, but some of the most effective color plans come from water colors. Monochromatic colors can be very restful, especially if teamed with coordinated equipment and fittings.

design themes

Just about anything goes. This is the one room in the house where you can indulge your fantasies and let your imagination run wild. Patterned tiles and towels can be a useful source of inspiration.

furnishings

Rarely do bathrooms have room for more furniture than a small table and chair. Tables can be a useful alternative to wall cabinets but bear in mind the effects of steam and condensation. Any medicines and toiletries should be kept locked away from young children. Blinds are the most popular window treatments for a bathroom, but don't overlook the possibility of using curtains in a large room. Walls are generally best painted to cope with condensation, and bold paint effects can look very dramatic in a large room and make a small room look larger.

details

Pictures may not fare well in a bathroom, so look for alternatives. Ceramics provide a decorative and practical alternative, and can be a good source of design inspiration too. Look around for interesting towels and bath mats, or items that may be designed for another purpose.

final touch

Replace your toilet with a modern style or one in an interesting color, or add a new toilet seat.

◁ The rough brick walls are painted in the same color to link the two textures. Simple shelving allows the brick to show through.

▷ The pale wood chairs and table co-ordinate with the floor and doors.

▽ A dramatic animal print provides both texture and pattern.

loft apartment

A multifunctional open-plan living space requires a different approach to interior design. More often than not, you are faced with a blank canvas and almost anything goes.

principles

Your first consideration should be to decide how to use the space. Are there just four blank walls or is the space already divided? If so, do these divisions fit your needs? Erase any preconceived thoughts and don't feel constrained by traditional room divisions. Walk around, viewing the space from all angles. What do you see as you enter the "front door"? It has the same effect as walking into the hall in a house, except the other "rooms" are all here too! In principle, the first areas you come to should be used for living and eating. Site your sleeping and bathing areas as far from the main door as possible to give some privacy and feeling of sleeping within your home as opposed to camping in the hallway.

lighting

One of the many plus points of loft living is the vast expanse of natural light. Think about whether your loft gets morning or evening light. Although natural light in large areas is a bonus during the day, large bare windows can create a very cold atmosphere at night. Allow for this when planning your furnishings. Artificial light must provide two functions. First, it must give good overhead lighting over a large area, and second, lower table lighting is necessary for a more intimate feel in the areas dedicated to relaxing and entertaining. In other words, every lighting eventuality must be provided for. The more flexible you make your lighting, the more you will be able to create the illusion of separate living areas.

floors

Loft floors have to be practical. Unless there is a natural division of space, it is better to use the same surface throughout. Wood is a popular choice, with rugs giving different moods and identifying separate areas. With high-tech living, textured rubber floors can look wonderful. One disadvantage is that they mark very easily, but if your loft is not subjected to a lot of use, this is easily compensated for by the fabulous range of colors and textures available.

color plan

Keep loft colors simple. Select a basic color and concentrate on using tone upon tone, reflected in different surfaces and textures, punctuated with dramatic accents. This is the one environment, with so much space available, where you can use really strong accent colors. If you have a very large space, you could try painting a corner in dark dramatic colors, but do make sure this balances with the colors used elsewhere.

design theme

Choose a theme that you can use in all different areas. Japanese minimal style suits loft living and is a good example of using a basic color with strong accents. Natural themes are a good choice, as the walls are often bare brick, and the neutral colors provide a good backdrop for a variety of accessories. Balance your ideas, as each area is going to have its own focal point.

furnishings

Organization is the word to remember when furnishing your loft apartment. You must work out what you have to fit in and where you are going to put it. Do you have space for floor-to-ceiling closets that will hide a multitude of sins? Think about how you are going to create individual room areas. Screens, blinds, even bookcases can all provide room dividers. If you live in a smaller studio, have you a space to store a folding table and chairs required only when you are entertaining? Most important, don't compromise on comfort, since you are working, resting and playing in the same space. Focus on blinds, shutters or nothing at all if you are high up above the roof-line.

details

Lofts love large, oversize accessories. A single lily in a large vase, for instance, is far more effective than a small arrangement of assorted flowers. A pair of large Chinese pots that would look too large on the floor in a standard house look fabulous on a table, dividing a living and eating area. Be selective with pictures. A large abstract oil painting can look very dramatic, but a simple option is to think of collecting contemporary photographs.

A large ceramic pot provides an attractive door stop, and the branches bring the outdoors inside.

Paint window frames and walls in different colors to define separate areas. Sofa beds are available in contemporary styles.

final touch

High-rise lofts lack a garden or even a view of one. Large ferns and even a simple window box of herbs in the kitchen area can all help to bring the garden indoors.

workspace

Working at home has many benefits. If you are to work and live in the same place, you need discipline and careful planning to prevent work encroaching on home life.

principles

Assess what your workspace is going to be used for. Are you running a business from home (check local regulations) or do you use the area to catch up on correspondence and household bills? Do you work alone or are you going to be sharing the room with someone else? If you have a choice of rooms and have a family at home, try to choose somewhere you will be least disturbed by noise and disruption. What kind of work do you do? If it is work that requires a lot of storage, this must be planned for at the outset. Nothing could be worse than having a stunning workspace with a mountain of papers that have no home! Ensure you have adequate ventilation, keep the window open as much as possible, and do take regular breaks. Time can pass by unnoticed when you work on your own and do not have anyone to remind you it's lunchtime. If you are using a computer, make sure it is placed in the right position to avoid eye and wrist strain.

◀ **Pale colors, metallic accessories and natural wood give this office a light and contemporary theme.**

▶ **Half-length shutters enable you to control light.**

lighting

Plan your lighting after you have decided what furniture you need and where it's going to be placed. Ensure you have sufficient lighting for the work you do, making sure there is no glare in your eyes, and no shadows are cast over the desk.

Try to avoid harsh neon strip lights if possible. An angle-poised lamp on the desk is a very useful supplement to complement overhead lighting; the lights can then be used together or separately, depending on the time of day and the work you are doing at that time.

floors

More often than not, a workspace at home ends up in the guest room, where you will have to keep the existing flooring. If starting from scratch, many of the principles applied to children's rooms are relevant here. Cork or vinyl floors are great if your work involves paints or moving your chair backwards and forwards from cabinets behind you. If choosing a carpet, think about carpet tiles. Not only are carpet tiles inexpensive and easy to lay, but if something spills, a new tile can easily be inserted without the expense involved in replacing an entire carpet. (Remember to add extra tiles when calculating the amounts required.)

color plan

The color you choose for a working environment must be one you feel totally happy with. Generally speaking, it is better to opt for calm coordinating colors. Bright, bold colors can be very distracting. In a small space dark colors can seem claustro-phobic. If you have to work in a room you dislike, place something in your favourite color on your desk to distract from the other colors around you. The secret is to close your eyes and imagine your perfect workspace. Open your eyes and find ways of achieving it in your own home.

◢ Roof slates are used on the cabinet doors as additional memo boards.

◗ Make functional shelves look attractive with decorative brackets.

design theme

Generally in an office, your profession will set the design theme. A designer will be surrounded by pattern which will give a very colorful "painterly" theme. An accountant will have an office full of files, which lends itself to a geometric design scheme.

furnishings

Functional furnishings are needed in a workspace. Try to make the maximum use of the space. If you can buy new furniture, buy from a specialty company that has storage solutions for small rooms. Sometimes the dimensions of manufactured furniture just don't fit, or the piece may be beyond your budget. Don't despair – a simple kitchen worktop cut to size will give you the maximum desk space and your work can be stored in filing cabinets below. Ensure, if possible, that you have a comfortable chair. Too often, chairs with no other place in the house end up in a home office. The only pattern in a workspace should come from a blind at the window or a cushion on your chair. Any other use of pattern can look fussy and distract from the discipline of work.

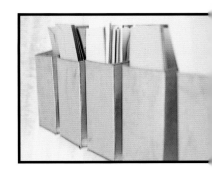

▶ _top_ Choose coordinating boxes to file catalogues and magazines.

▶ A tall wooden drawer unit blends in with the unusual carved worktop.

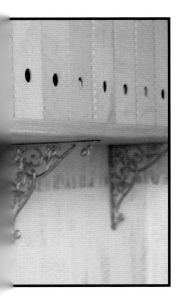

details

Workspace details must always have a function. Look for interesting filing boxes and filing trays for your desk. Offices cannot survive without memo boards and you can never have too many! Use extra wall space to display any certificates or pictures or work you are proud of. These serve as a great reminder to the solo worker at home of what he or she has achieved.

final touch

Special photos will remind you that there is life beyond the office.

sunroom

Not everyone is fortunate enough to have a garden. Even for those who do, many days pass without being able to go outside and enjoy being surrounded by plants and nature. First designed by the Victorians as "winter gardens", a conservatory or sunroom brings the atmosphere of a garden into your home.

principles

Work out how you are going to use your sunroom. Is it to be used as a sitting room, or will you also use it as a dining room? Would you like to use it in the evenings?

The design of a sunroom must be sympathetic to the architecture of your house and you should give careful consideration to how it relates to the room from which it leads.

Trailing ivy around a verdigris wall light echoes the garden theme.

Pale terra-cotta and green paintwork is echoed in a terra-cotta floor with green accent lines.

Exterior wood-work is painted green to co-ordinate.

Plants thrive in sunroom conditions, but do make sure there is a source of water nearby for easy watering. Check you have adequate ventilation and heating for both you and the plants. Take steps to prevent condensation, especially if the sunroom is adjacent to a kitchen. Rain outside is one thing, but do not give yourself this problem when you have brought the garden inside!

lighting

Sunrooms cannot rely solely on natural light. A large glass roof gives the room an unrivaled light, airy feel, but this must be supplemented by artificial light for evening and winter use. Position outlets and switches carefully to avoid danger when watering. You could use fittings designed for bathroom use. The most effective solution is to use wall lights or spotlights that can be attached to a high window frame.

floors

Bear in mind that sunroom floors have to be practical. The surface should reflect the natural garden theme, and rugs (with nonslip underlay) bridge the gap between home and garden. Vinyl flooring is available in a large variety of natural effects and terra-cotta floor tiles win the prize for the ultimate in conservatory flooring, looking great in any design scheme.

color plan

Use garden colors in your sunroom and you can't go wrong. Having said that, a garden has a huge range of colors so think carefully about what kind of garden you would like to create. Use gardening books for inspiration and limit your colors to a particular theme or style. Pinks and greens conjure up visions of an English country garden, whereas lots of leafy green plants and bright colors can transport you to the tropics. Focus on the color for the window frames as these will form a dominant part of your color scheme.

 **A stable door connects the sunroom to the kitchen. The sofa is positioned to look out over the garden.**

The lion's head placed on an end wall makes an unusual feature.

design theme

Gardening books can help you choose the right colors and themes to suit your room: Mediterranean, Japanese, Californian, Italian, formal – whichever you choose, try to ensure that it works with the rest of your home. However, not everyone wants to create an inside garden in their sunroom, especially if the room is to be used for a specific function. Look at the room it leads off and take inspiration from the decoration within the house.

furnishings

In keeping with the garden principle, furnishings made from natural fabrics, especially wicker and wood, suit sunroom living. Keep soft furnishings simple and avoid curtains. Blinds suit the lines of a sunroom and provide shade and insulation that you can control.

Most of the wall area is likely to be glass and any solid walls are likely to be the original walls of the house. Brick walls can look very attractive but you could also paint them. Experiment with paint effects that enhance brickwork.

details

Look for quirky accessories to give your sunroom an individual look. The view outside provides the main backdrop, so pictures are rarely required. Bringing the outside in creates a large-scale effect, which can be used to best effect with large, overscale ornaments. Sculpture is especially striking, and echoes the theme of garden statues.

final touch

Complete the garden mood with a small decorative fountain – running water is the ultimate sound for relaxation.

109

troubleshooting

◗ how can I make a low ceiling look higher?

The key to making awkward low ceilings look higher is to paint the walls and ceiling the same color. Ideally this should be a pale, flat color. With no contrast between the ceiling and wall, the illusion of a higher room is created. Also, try to keep all your furniture to one style. If the room is a dark color, rich wood looks particularly effective.

extra tip! Hanging pictures lower than usual gives the illusion of a higher ceiling.

◗ how can I make a high ceiling look lower?

High ceilings in narrow rooms can often make the room look out of proportion. High walls can take strong, dark colors. Paint the ceiling white, and the contrast has the effect of lowering the ceiling height. Dark furniture balances the dark wall color and a picture rail painted white adds to the illusion of a lower wall.

extra tip! White curtains and a white fireplace give additional impact to the contrast of dark and pale colors.

▶ how can I decorate a paneled room?

Paneling is a wonderful feature. Emphasize the richness of the paneling by making sure the room decor is kept very simple, plain and uncluttered. Disciplined use of pattern and color will add interest to the room. This can be achieved by a simple patchwork quilt on the bed.

extra tip! Paneled rooms often have window seats. Make a feature of these by using cushions to create an inexpensive and useful seating area. You could also convert the seating to include underseat storage to keep clutter to a minimum.

▶ how do I decorate a room with partially paneled walls?

Balance the two surfaces by painting the ceiling a color that works with both surfaces. Link the shade to the wall color. Natural colors that echo the wood tones work well. The use of wooden furniture or accessories will bring the wood wall into the room.

extra tip! Painting a stencil on the ceiling forms an additional link between the two walls.

how can I make a small room look larger?

A great way to make a small room look larger, especially one with no natural light, is to use spotlights recessed into the ceiling and reflected into a mirror. This creates the illusion of double the space. You must, however, use a mirror across the whole wall to get this effect.

extra tip! A wall of tiles from the tub across to the sink area will make a bathroom look wider.

how can I take advantage of lots of light?

If you are lucky enough to have a room that benefits from lots of natural light, use the space that would have had a central pendant light to have a decorative candle holder. You will only need to use it late in the evening when it will provide a wonderful light. It will also make an attractive focal point during the day. This is ideal for a dining room that isn't used during the day. Using pale colors on the walls and curtains will make the room look even lighter.

extra tip! Valances work best used on large windows, providing a frame with minimal loss of light.

▶ how can I give a traditional room a contemporary feel?

Disguise the traditional features of the room by painting the walls in a pale color. Use plain simple furniture that does not fight with the traditional "bones" of the room. To create the contemporary feel, choose strong contemporary designs for selected soft furnishings.

extra tip! Keep accessories to a minimum to create a contemporary look.

▶ how can I make a featureless, modern room look interesting?

When you have a plain empty box for a room, try painting the walls two contrasting colors. A room needs a focal point to add interest. By hanging chic modern lighting from the ceiling, this creates an effective focal point. You could also include interesting, sculptural plants, such as orchids, which look stunning against a plain background.

extra tip! Choose accessories that work well with the two wall colors. This will bring the whole room together.

○ I want to open up the wall between my kitchen and dining room. How can I make it look interesting?

Linking two rooms together increases a feeling of space. The wall here has been made a feature in its own right with recesses for displaying beautiful pieces of ceramic.

extra tip! Emphasize the geometric lines by hanging long narrow pictures alongside a rectangular table and tall chairs.

○ what curtains can I use for a tall window?

The use of curtains on tall, narrow windows can overpower a room. A good solution is to use two sets of shutters. By keeping one set open and one set shut, you can create the illusion of smaller windows.

extra tip! Placing the tub in the center of the room makes the walls on either side look wider.

○ how can I hide my child's bed in the daytime?

By choosing a Native American theme for the room, you can hide the bed disguised as a tent. Paint the room in strong colors, including the ceiling. Link the tent pattern with the fabric used for the window blinds to ensure it feels part of the overall scheme.

◐ can I use white curtains at a wide window without overpowering the room?

By painting and furnishing the room in white and pale tones, the curtains blend into the decorating scheme. All pale-colored rooms should always be anchored by a darker color to create contrast. Here, this function is fulfilled by the antique iron bed.

extra tip! To give additional color contrast, try lining the curtains in a pale color which is revealed when the curtains are drawn back.

◐ how can I fit a table into a small room?

In small rooms especially, every inch of space has to be used. By cutting a piece of wood to fit around this awkward wall, a table is created, using minimal space and utilizing an area that could otherwise have been difficult to furnish. You could also think about using a fold-down table and foldaway chair.

extra tip! Painting the woodwork the same color as the walls makes a small room feel larger.

○ how can I make my old bedroom armoire look different?

If you want to update an item of furniture, rather than replace it, you could use plain wood doors and cover them with a themed wallpaper. The "books" paper used here creates the illusion of a library bookshelf rather than an armoire and gives a lived-in feel to a minimal, contemporary-style room.

extra tip! The dark book spines are highlighted by the use of dark bedlinen.

○ how can I fit a second bed in a small guest room?

Two beds in a small room can look very cramped especially if they are not required all the time. A neat solution is to buy a bed that hides the second bed underneath.

extra tip! Placing the bed in the center of the room can make a small room look longer.

◖ how can I incorporate ceiling beams into my decorating scheme?

Balancing the colors used is the key to incorporating the beams into the overall color scheme. Start by painting the walls and ceiling in one color. The beams and all the woodwork should then be painted in a second color.

extra tip! Accent the checkered effect of the ceiling and window panes with check fabrics.

◖ I want a dramatic black bathroom, but how can I avoid making an expensive mistake?

To use a dark color effectively, especially in a small space, it must be carefully balanced with a contrasting color. White works especially well with black. Make sure there is a balance of color in the room scheme.

◦ how can I transform my boring white kitchen units?

Be bold! Use the units as a blank canvas, and paint large squares over the entire area. You could base your design on a fabric pattern, and then use the fabric on chairs to link the scheme together.

extra tip! Using white tiles makes the wall area blend in with the background color of the units background color.

◦ how can I transform an old cupboard?

Old furniture in poor condition can be difficult to paint. Create a decoupage effect by covering the cupboard in sheets of music. This will cover the old surface and give an unusual and inexpensive facelift to the cupboard.

extra tip! Varnish the completed work. This both protects the paper and gives the cupboard an antique effect.

◀ how can I improve the look of an old fireplace?

Give new life to an old fireplace by using tiles on the actual surround, rather than the traditional way on the side panels. Large thick tiles can give a wonderful Mediterranean feel to a room.

extra tip! Painting the walls in a strong color makes the tiles look even more effective!

▶ what door can I use in an unusual room?

If you have rooms with unusual features, look at ways to enhance them. Create a door that echoes the shape of the ceiling. Not only does this look wonderful, but it reduces the expanse of wall area.

extra tip! Pictures hung at different levels draw the eye up the wall.

◀ how can I create more storage space?

The wall space between the cabinet and the sink here is not quite big enough for another cabinet, but the space is wide enough for shelves, which can be used for books, as well as essentials.

how can I use pattern on high walls?

A geometric design works well over large or high wall areas as it will not dominate the room. Using the wall as a grid, a painted trellis pattern gives soft lines. A stenciled or stamped motif in the center of each diamond gives the illusion of a smaller pattern.

extra tip!   Paint an old piece of furniture to coordinate with the walls.

how can I update unfashionable fabrics?

If you have duvet covers, curtains or upholstery that you can't afford to replace, treat your room to a new coat of paint. When updating decorating schemes, the temptation can be to add something totally different. Instead, emphasize any existing design, in this case, checks, by painting the walls in bright bold yellow checks.

extra tip!   Balance the colors and update the existing curtains by applying a blue edging.

◑ how can I decorate my small attic room?

Vertical stripes have the effect of making an area look higher and therefore more spacious – ideal for an attic room. This will also provide pattern and interest without overpowering a small area. Give the space character with decorative furniture and accessories.

extra tip! A large picture on a small wall can make the space seem larger.

◑ how can I give my mirror a new look?

Mirrors tend to be used alone or with small frames. Break the rules! Fix the mirror on the wall unframed, and paint a wide border on the wall to give an unusual wall effect. With such a large expanse of white, choose your accessories to blend in with the mirror edging for an uncluttered look.

extra tip! Always check the reflection before placing a large mirror on a wall – make sure it isn't revealing anything embarrassing.

can I re-cover a chair without spending a fortune?

The easiest way to re-cover a chair without spending a fortune is to find a throw, and drape this over the chair. Not only does it look stunning but it can be easily changed in the future. This informal look suits both modern and traditional interiors. This is particularly useful to ring the changes between the seasons.

extra tip! Choose a patterned throw for a plain chair or a plain throw for a patterned upholstery fabric.

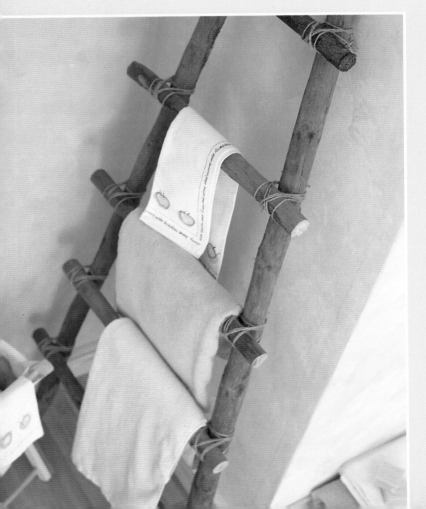

I don't like ordinary towel rails. How can I hang my towels?

A wooden ladder is a stylish and inexpensive way to both hang your towels, and create a natural look in the bathroom. You can also find striking minimalist designs made from metal tubing.

extra tip! Buy towels in coordinating toning colors, rather than several towels of the same color.

○ what can I do with an old wooden floor if I don't want to use carpet?

Be brave, and paint the floor. Checks are easy to do especially if you only use one color. By using a woodwash, the natural wood shows through the colored squares. Diagonal checks also make a room look larger.

extra tip! Keep to a harmonious color scheme which will link the fireplace with the fabrics and floor.

○ I like white walls and wooden floors, but how can I add a splash of color to my room?

Place a brightly colored rug at the entrance. This is the first thing people see as they come in and can be very useful for absorbing noise on a wooden floor. You will need to add a nonslip underlay for safety. Bear in mind that the rug will become soiled in this location.

extra tip! By painting the outside of the front door in a strong color, you get the feeling of color before you enter the house.

measurement guide

GUIDE TO NUMBER OF TILES TO USE

Tile size	Tiles per square yard (square meter)
4 x 4 in (10 x 10 cm)	81 (100)
4 x 8 in (10 x 20 cm)	45 (50)
6 x 6 in (15 x 15 cm)	36 (44)
8 x 8 in (20 x 20 cm)	25 (25)

CURTAIN FABRIC

To calculate how much fabric is required for curtains, first determine the length, then the width of the area you wish to cover.

Length
1. Measure the height of the window from the curtain rod to the floor (or the level you wish the curtains to reach).
2. Add approximately 10 in/25 cm for finishing both the top and bottom hems.

Width
1. For gathered curtains, measure the width of your window and mutliply by 2.
2. Add 2 in/5 cm for each side hem of each curtain, whether you are going to have one, two or more curtains.
3. Most fabrics come in a standard width (often 45 in/1.2 m) so you may need two lengths of fabric to make one curtain.
4. Divide the total width by the standard width to see how many lengths you will require.

Note: If using patterned material, make sure that where the lengths are joined the pattern matches up. (You might have to buy extra fabric to allow for this.)

PAINT COVERAGE

Surface areas paint will cover:

1 quart latex	130sq.ft/12 sq.mtrs
1 gallon latex	400sq.ft/38 sq.mtrs
1 gallon primer	500sq.ft/46 sq.mtrs

CARPETS

1. Measure the room to be carpeted, making a rough plan and noting your measurements on it.
2. Calculate the maximum width and length that are required to cover the space.
3. Multiply the maximum length by the maximum width.

For example:
$$3 \times 5.5 = 16.5 \text{ sq. yd.}$$

4. For budgeting purposes, you can now estimate the costs of the carpet by multiplying this figure by the price per square foot (meter).

$$16.5 \times £21 = \$346.50$$

Measuring and budgeting for carpets
Always measure for the maximum amount of carpet required, even it it means that some carpet will be wasted. Remember to include doorway spaces.

Note: Never mix calculations using metric and U.S. measurements. Always ask a professional to verify your measurements before placing an order.

retail sources

WALLPAPERING

The approximate number of bolts required according to room circumference and wall height, is shown in bold. 1 bolt = 2 single rolls. Deduct one single roll for every two regular-size doors or windows.

Room circumference in feet (meters)	Ceiling height in feet (meters)				
	8 (2.5)	9 (2.75)	10 (3)	11 (3.35)	12 (3.66)
28 (8.5)	5	6	7	7	8
30 (9)	5	6	7	8	9
32 (9.8)	6	7	7	8	9
34 (10.4)	7	7	8	9	10
36 (11)	7	7	8	9	10
38 (11.6)	7	8	9	10	11
40 (12.2)	7	8	9	10	11
42 (12.8)	8	9	9	11	12
44 (13.4)	8	9	10	11	12
48 (14.6)	9	10	10	12	13
52 (15.8)	9	11	12	13	14
60 (18.3)	11	12	13	15	16
68 (20.7)	12	14	15	16	18
72 (22)	13	14	16	18	20

ABC Carpet & Home
888 Broadway
New York, NY 10003
(212) 473-3000; stores also in CA, DC, MD, NJ, PA
Furnishings, rugs, bedlinens, accessories

American Blind and Wallpaper Factory
(800) 575-8016
www.abwf.com
Name-brand window and wall treatments at discount, online or mail order

Bed, Bath & Beyond
620 Avenue of the Americas
New York, NY 10011
(800) GO-BEYOND
www.bedbath.com
Furnishings, kitchenware, accessories

Benjamin Moore
(800) 826-2623 for store locations
www.benjaminmoore.com
Paints, wallpaper, decorative finishes

Bombay Company
(800) 829-7789 for store locations
www.bombayco.com
Furnishings, accessories

Crate and Barrel
(800) 323-5461 for store locations
Furnishings, linens, storage, accessories
www.crateandbarrel.com

Domain Home Furnishings
(800) 4-DOMAIN for store locations
www.domain-home.com

Furniture.com
(888) 225-2251 for design consultants, or order online
www.furniture.com
Furnishings, lighting, rugs, accessories

Home Depot
(800) 430-3376 for store locations
www.homedepot.com

IKEA
(888) 225-4532 for store locations
www.ikea.com
Scandinavian furnishings and decorative items

Pier One
(800) 447-1610 for store locations
Furnishings storage, kitchenware, accessories

Pottery Barn
(800) 922-5507 for store locations
Furnishings, storage, kitchenware, accessories

Sherwin Williams
(800) 622-8468 for store locations
Paints, wallpapers

Smith & Hawken
(800) 776-3336 for store locations
www.smith-hawken.com
Indoor and outdoor furnishings

Williams Sonoma
(800) 541-2233 for store locations
Kitchenware, cookware, small appliances

professional organizations

American Institute of Architects
1735 New York Avenue NW
Washington, DC 20006
(202) 626-7300
www.aiaonline.com

American Society of Interior Designers
608 Massachusetts Avenue NE
Washington, DC 20002
(202) 546-3480, or (800) 775-ASID for a designer referral
www.asid.org

picture credits

index